The Tortilla Book

Also by Diana Kennedy:

THE CUISINES OF MEXICO

DIANA KENNEDY

The Tortilla Book

Drawings by Sidonie Coryn

HARPER & ROW, PUBLISHERS
New York, Hagerstown
San Francisco
London

For Lily May

Designed by Gloria Adelson

Library of Congress Cataloging in Publication Data

Kennedy, Diana.
  The tortilla book.
  Bibliography: p.
  Includes index.
  1. Tortillas. I. Title.
TX770.K46 1975   641.8′2   75-6343
ISBN 0-06-012346-X
ISBN 0-06-012347-8 pbk.

83 84 85 86   10 9 8

Contents

Illustrations

Acknowledgments

For this collection of recipes, which can be found in existing Mexican cookbooks in Spanish, listed in the bibliography, I have drawn heavily on the books by Josefina Velázquez de León, who was perhaps the only person who has traveled to the principal Mexican towns in the provinces giving cooking lessons and at the same time collecting local recipes. I acknowledge my debt to her with grateful thanks. To Frances McCullough, a very special friend and editor, I also extend my deep thanks for her contagious and continued enthusiasm and appreciation.

I should also like to thank Valerie Marchant for reading the manuscript and for her valuable suggestions; Gloria Adelson, who designed the book; and Margery Tippie, who not only edits my copy but cooks through my books with such pleasure and enthusiasm.

Introduction

Whenever the subject of Mexican food comes up, French chefs look supercilious, the Spaniards look down their noses, and the Italians smile politely—don't they know there is a world of difference between the real thing and what predictably turns up as Mexican food in so-called authentic restaurants, fast-food chains, and in cans and frozen packages in every supermarket? But in spite of it all, Mexican food is a firmly established favorite, and it is not an exaggeration to say that millions of tortillas are made and distributed daily throughout the United States.

What is a tortilla? A round, thin "pancake" of unleavened corn dough (I am not including in this book the wheat-flour tortillas of northern Mexico) that has been prepared and eaten in Mexico from the earliest times until the present day. Parched corn kernels are briefly cooked in a solution of unslaked lime and water and then left to soak until they are soft enough to be ground to a smooth dough, or *masa*. The tortillas are then formed by one of several methods. In many parts of Mexico today the dough is still patted out between the hands. In some of the coastal regions and in the south of Mexico, on the other hand, the dough is patted out onto a large piece of banana leaf or polyethylene wrap with one hand, while the other turns the wrap rhythmically clockwise. But the easiest way of making tortillas—that of stamping them out with a metal or wooden tortilla press—is winning hands down. The tortilla is then cooked on a hot, ungreased griddle until it is slightly speckled with brown but still soft and pliable.

Eating tortillas for the first time, you may wonder what the fuss is all about —in other words, they may leave you cold. Then one day you will begin to crave one; unconsciously they will have become a passion, an addiction for life.

This is not meant to be a "compleat" or definitive book encompassing all the regional variations of the *taco* and *enchilada* ad infinitum, but a small selection from the hundreds of versions both known and rare. It is a "how-to" book designed to show that interesting and unexpected dishes can be concocted from tortillas—fresh, stale, and dried out to a crisp—with a minimum of basic equipment and exotic ingredients.

I learned very quickly during my years in Mexico that a tortilla is never thrown away. While still fresh and pliable it is eaten as bread is in other cuisines; it actually becomes an edible spoon accompanying practically all Mexican dishes. Wrapped around small pieces of meat, vegetables, and cheese, and seasoned with any one of a hundred *picante* sauces, it becomes a *taco* in its simplest form. Slightly stale, cut into triangles, and fried crisp, it becomes a scoop—*totopo* or *tostadita*—for *guacamole* or fried beans. In crisp little squares it makes croutons for soup. Again, stale and dried, cut into pieces, and lightly fried, it can be tossed into a sauce, cooked briefly and garnished lavishly to become *chilaquiles*—an entrancing name meaning, literally, "pieces of broken-up old sombrero." Or the same might be used like pasta in a casserole to form the layers between meat, vegetables, cheese, and cream often liberally doused with a tomato sauce to become the "dry soups" (*sopas secas*) or savory puddings (*budines*) so dear to the Mexican's heart and stomach. Or, prepared in the same way, dropped into soups to thicken and lend an elusive corn flavor.

Whole tortillas can be fried quite flat and smothered with a paste of fried beans, topped with shredded meats and crisp salad so that they become an edible plate—a *tostada*—a great favorite among Mexicans and non-Mexicans alike. Even when the tortilla is dried out to a crisp, and you may think that it has had its day, it can be ground up to form a dough for little round, fat cakes —*gordas*—or savory balls—*bolitos*—to drop into the soup. Then, to take the tortilla at every stage, the raw corn dough can be used either alone, or mixed with cheese, potatoes, or chilies, and transformed by some simple alchemy to produce any one of the *antojitos* (lit., "little whims"), among them *quesadillas, sopes, garnachas, chalupas*—to nibble on at any time of day or night. In fact, in culinary terms the tortilla can do almost anything, and is perhaps the most versatile piece of foodstuff the world has ever known.

An accident that forced me to cancel my usual summer wanderings in Mexico led me instead to reread my notebooks of years gone by and my collection of regional cookbooks in Spanish that I had virtually ignored until then. I became very hungry, so very soon the recipes that follow became a reality.

Many of the recipes can be produced on a very low budget; many are vegetarian; and there are some for skinny as well as rich diets. They can be bland, mildly spicy, or downright hot, whatever you choose. Some of the dishes, with their luxuriant garnishes—to be eaten as well as looked at—are a meal in themselves. Many are cooked and served in the same dish. And although there are often many component parts that make the preparation look complicated, there is a lot that can be done ahead—sauces can be prepared and frozen—while the assembling and comparatively brief cooking can be done at the last moment.

A Note to the Cook

How often I have heard the complaint, "When I make *enchiladas*, the tortillas always fall apart," or "The tortillas break as I roll them up for *tacos*"! I have tried to anticipate these points with rather long and detailed notes at the beginning of each section dealing with a particular group of recipes, that is, *tacos*, *enchiladas* (methods I and II), *chilaquiles*, and so on. Unfortunately, most cooks won't take a few extra moments before launching into a foreign cuisine to read the additional information to the recipe instructions. Often detailed methods, dos and don'ts, cannot be repeated a hundred times over. So, if you want to cook something really well, *read!*

As I have said elsewhere, this is a collection of recipes from Mexican sources. I have merely *adjusted* the recipes (how I hate that word "adapt," which is responsible for so many of the horrible things that have happened to ethnic foods in this country), sometimes suggesting a slightly different cooking method to suit our utensils and stoves or more realistic quantities of ingredients and an occasional substitution.

There are many notable and deliberate omissions. For instance, I have not included wheat-flour tortillas or recipes for *burritos* and *chivichangas*, for which they are used. Nor will you find the Mexicans' favorite *quesadillas* stuffed with squash flowers or corn fungus, for these call for more exotic ingredients, which are outside the scope of this book. For information on them you would have to turn to my *Cuisines of Mexico*.

Utensils

This is simple cooking, and no equipment that is not found in most kitchens is really necessary. However, you will be using the following a great deal, so may I recommend:

BLENDER—It is much easier to handle and clean a blender jar that has a detachable bottom—pieces of dried chili are likely to get caught in the blades. For Mexican cooking calling for a lot of different sauces, *two* blender jars and sets of blades are ideal. Always choose a heavy-duty blender.

FRYING PANS—Nothing works quite like a heavy cast-iron pan for this type of cooking, in which sauces are reduced over a rather high flame. The ideal would be three pans—8, 9, and 10 inches in diameter at the top. In an *enchilada* recipe, for example, often filling and sauce will be cooking simultaneously—and then you will have the tortillas to fry.

GRIDDLE—A cast-iron griddle is helpful; if you don't have one, use a heavy frying pan (see above).

KNIVES—A 10-inch carbon-steel French chef's knife or Chinese cleaver, for fast chopping, and a 3½-inch paring knife are most suitable.

SPLATTERPROOF COVER—It is a good idea to have a lid of this sort, since sauces are cooked over a high flame and tend to splatter, especially when they have a ground chili base—then they are heavy and splatter ferociously.

SERVING DISHES—I have purposely cooked and served these recipes in the minimum number and simplest of dishes. Ovenproof serving dishes are ideal, and the following sizes should serve as a guide: 13½ x 9 x 2, 8 x 8 x 2, 5½ x 9½ x 3.

TONGS—Ordinary metal kitchen tongs are the best, nothing with serrated or fluted ends that could tear the tortillas.

TORTILLA PRESS—Not an essential unless you intend to make your own tortillas. I recommend a press with a 6½-inch-diameter plate. (See Sources for Mexican Ingredients, pages 149-152.)

Ingredients

AVOCADOS

The avocado is one of those delightfully all-purpose trees. Not only is it beautifully decorative with its glossy, dark-green leaves and abundant fruit hanging like large fat pears, but practically every part of it is edible. The leaves, for instance, can be cooked with barbecues or *tamales*; or they can be lightly toasted, ground, and added to a *pipián* (a stew thickened with ground nuts or seeds) or fried beans. The thin skin of the small, black avocado grown in Mexico can be mashed with the flesh to give a rather special texture and anisey flavor. And, if you are not going to use the pit to grow another tree, then let it dry and grate a little of it into an *enchilada* sauce—as it is used in northern Mexico—but not too much, or the sauce will be quite bitter.

If you are not living in an area where avocados are grown, never wait to buy until the day you want to use them. You can so very rarely find a ripe one. It is much safer to anticipate two or three days ahead and let them ripen in a warm spot in the kitchen. A good, ripe avocado should be tender at the stalk base, but not too soft, to the touch; the pit should not rattle about inside as you shake it, and the skin should not have parted from the flesh. When opened, the flesh itself should be compact and shiny, like firm butter, and have a rich anisey,

15

hazelnut flavor. Those sold in markets throughout the East vary enormously in quality, and so often the only ones available are the large, roundish bright green avocados with thick, woody skin and flesh that is watery, sweet, and tasteless. The California avocados—which are smaller, with a coarse, blackish skin —come into season in February and are far superior.

It is always advisable to cut the avocado open and scoop out the flesh with a wooden spoon. Trying to peel one is a messy job at best, and the scooping method probably reduces discoloration.

How often have you tried to cut a peeled avocado into neat slices as it slithers around in your hand? Well, don't peel it first. Insert the point of a sharp, stainless-steel paring knife through the skin and flesh at the bulbous base of the avocado and make a vertical incision down to the stalk end. Make parallel incisions—cutting right through to the pit—all the way around. Then peel the skin off each slice and ease it out with the point of the knife.

The last step should be done at the last moment, but you can do the vertical cutting ahead of time and then wrap the avocado tightly in polyethylene wrap, ready to skin and use later.

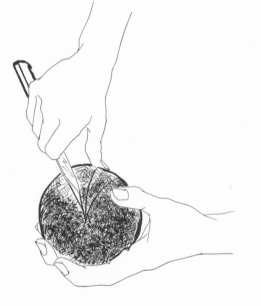

Slicing an avocado

BEANS

—•••—

Black, pinto, and California pink beans are recommended for these recipes. They are available in practically any supermarket throughout the country.

Beans are an essential part of any Mexican meal. They have a great natural flavor, and good, careful cooking enhances it. I always think they taste much better cooked in an earthenware bean pot, but this is not essential—especially if you are going to refry the beans later.

Some dos and don'ts

No matter how carefully the beans have been packed, you do need to rinse them briefly and go through them carefully to make sure that no small stones or pieces of earth may have been left in.

Do not soak the beans ahead of time; soaking impairs the flavor. But if you have done so, then don't throw the water away; cook the beans in it.

Don't add salt until the beans are almost done. It is said to harden the skins if added at the beginning of the cooking time.

The amount of liquid and cooking time can only be given approximately. The quality of the beans, the size and material of the pot affects these factors.

Beans always have a better flavor the day after they have been cooked.

They must be refrigerated after cooking, or they will turn sour very quickly.

When cooked, they can be frozen and stored.

Pot Beans *(Pinto, Pink)*

1 pound pinto or pink beans
12 to 14 cups cold water
2 tablespoons lard or peanut or safflower oil
¼ medium onion, roughly chopped

Cover the beans with the water; add the lard and onion and bring to a boil, then cover the pan and simmer until the skins are soft and breaking open (about 1½ hours).

1 tablespoon salt

Add the salt and simmer for another 30 minutes, or until the beans are thoroughly soft. There should be plenty of broth.

Pot Beans (*Black*)

1 pound black beans
10 to 12 cups cold water
2 tablespoons lard or
    peanut or safflower
    oil
¼ medium onion,
    roughly chopped
	Cover the beans with the water. Add the lard and onion and bring to a boil, then cover the pan and simmer until the skins are soft and breaking open (about 1½ to 2 hours).

1 tablespoon salt, or to
    taste
2 sprigs *epazote*
    (optional)
	Add the salt and *epazote* and simmer for another 45 minutes. When cooked the beans should be soft, almost mushy, and there should be plenty of broth.

To most Mexicans, to cook black beans without *epazote* is unthinkable. It does add an elusive and delicious flavor to them.

Refried Beans

A slightly rough "paste" of mashed and fried beans is so often a part of or garnish for, Mexican snacks. As a general rule, and I won't go into the few regional exceptions, the beans are fried without additional flavoring—even onion is frowned on in some parts of the country. To get the very best-flavored beans, fry them with good-quality pork lard, but do not use bacon fat, which is too strong.

A heavy 10-inch frying pan is the ideal utensil for frying this quantity, which will produce about 2½ cups of bean paste. A word of caution: blend the beans in two or three lots, and if the mixture in the blender is hot, keep your hand firmly on the lid when the machine is switched on.

A blender
½ pound cooked beans
    (beans and broth to-
    gether should meas-
    ure about 4 cups)
	Put some of the beans and broth into the blender and blend for a few seconds until you have a rough puree. Blend the rest in the same way.

A frying pan
5 tablespoons lard or vegetable oil
¼ medium onion, finely chopped
The bean puree

Heat the lard and cook the onion gently, without browning, until it is soft. Add the bean puree, little by little, and cook it over a fairly high flame until it starts to dry out to a thick consistency. Keep scraping the bottom and sides of the pan as the beans cook so that the crusty bits are well incorporated and do not stick and burn.

The beans are now ready to be used, or stored or frozen.

CHEESE

The most commonly used cheeses in Mexico for these recipes are *añejo* (aged), and *queso fresco* (fresh cheese).

Añejo is a dry, salty cheese that crumbles easily and is used mostly for garnishing and for cooking in *enchiladas*, *chilaquiles*, and so on. I personally don't like its harshness when cooked, and would almost always prefer to use *queso fresco*. When it is called for in garnishes I have suggested Romano, finely grated (but not the one that is already grated and packaged), or the Argentinian Parmesan-type cheese called Sardo, which is more moderately priced.

Queso fresco is a white, crumbly, moist cheese made for family consumption in every little ranch in Mexico. The *queso blanco* generally sold in Latin-American markets looks as though it might do but is not a good product. It is preferable to use a good-quality, loose farmer cheese, which when well salted and mixed with chopped onion makes a delicious filling for *enchiladas*.

Queso Chihuahua is a mild, spongy, pale yellow cheese, made in great wheels by the Mennonites in the state of Chihuahua, that rather resembles a mild Cheddar. Suggested substitutes: mild Cheddar; mild, block Muenster; jack.

Queso ranchero is a dry, salty cheese used on *antojitos* in some parts of Mexico. Moderately-priced Sardo or Romano is a good substitute.

CHILIES, CANNED

Chipotles en escabeche or *en adobo* are carried by many stores specializing in Mexican food. The *chipotle* is actually the *chile jalapeño* dried and smoked, which gives it its curious tobacco-y flavor. Fiery hot in the can, they should be used with discretion in soups and sauces.

Jalapeños en escabeche are perhaps the best known of all the chilies to lovers of Mexican food. They are sold very widely throughout the United States, and can nearly always be found in the now-ubiquitous Mexican food section in practically any supermarket. They are most often used as a garnish or condiment. They have their own special flavor, and can vary from fairly to burning hot.

Canned peeled green chilies. See Anaheim or Californian chili, page 21.

CHILIES, DRIED

Ancho, a wrinkled, deep reddish-brown chili, actually the *poblano* ripened and dried; it can vary from mild to hot. Broad, as its name implies, a good average sample could be about 5 inches long and 3 inches wide at its broadest part. The size should be taken into consideration when calculating the amount to be used in any given recipe. If four are called for and the chilies are much smaller than this average size, then make up the difference with one or two extra small ones.

Pasilla, a long, narrow, black-hued chili. Rounded at its tip and with a wrinkled, ridged surface, a good average size would be 6 by 1 inches. It has a delicious flavor and is quite mild—until you come across the very hot veins and seeds clustered at the stem end.

New Mexican (chile de ristra) is a reddish-brown, smooth-skinned chili—the dried Anaheim or Californian. A good average one measures 4½ by 1¼ inches, and can vary from mild to hot. It does not have a very rich flavor—like that of the *ancho,* for instance—and is used only in some of the northern states of Mexico.

Storage of dried chilies

Providing they were not damp or worm or moth ridden in the first place, dried chilies will keep almost indefinitely if stored in a cool, dry place. Even then it is advisable to go through them every few months and throw out any that may be deteriorating.

CHILIES, FRESH

Jalapeños, smooth-skinned, mid-green chilies. Generally a little darker than the *serranos* (see below), they are distributed quite widely throughout the United

States. An average-sized one would be about 2½ inches long and ¾ inch wide. It has a very special flavor when cooked, and can only be substituted for—rather unsatisfactorily—by another fresh green chili that is perhaps more readily available, not by a canned one. It can vary from hot to very hot.

Poblano, a long, triangular-shaped chili with a dark-green, undulating surface. An average-size one would measure 5 by 3 inches, although out of season they tend to be much smaller. They are used after they have been charred and peeled, although sometimes in the northwest they are fried and peeled. This tends to be a much more messy method of dealing with them, and does not enhance the natural flavor of the chilies as charring them does. In the United States they are available in Washington, Chicago, and throughout the Southwest.

A substitute would be the *Anaheim or Californian chili*. This is a long, thin, mid-green chili that is widely distributed in the Southwest. It is charred and peeled in exactly the same way as the *chile poblano* (see page 30 for preparation of chili strips), and is probably better known as "canned peeled green chili." It can vary from hot to mild. The seeds should be removed before using them.

Chile serrano. This is a smooth-skinned, mid-green chili with an average size of 1½ inches in length and just under ½ inch in width. Although very hot, it has a distinctive flavor, and is generally available in the same places as the *chile poblano*. Elsewhere you will have to substitute the long, skinny green chili that is available the year round in Chinese, Caribbean, or Italian markets. When a recipe calls for fresh chilies, never used canned ones—they will alter the flavor and texture of the food.

Storage of fresh chilies

Fresh chilies can be stored in the refrigerator up to three weeks with proper care. They should be wrapped in paper toweling and stored in paper bags (not polyethylene, which makes them sweat and deteriorate quickly). They tend, of course, to become a little wrinkled and lose a little of their fresh, sharp flavor; but they will do.

From time to time you should go through them, separating those that are turning color—they go from green, to yellow, and then red as they ripen—for immediate use and throw away any that have become overripe and mushy. If they are frozen when they are fresh and uncooked, they lose their flavor and texture, which is so important in such things as fresh sauces and scrambled eggs. There are some cooked sauces, however, that call for the chilies to be broiled or boiled; for those you could cook the *serranos* and then freeze them.

CHORIZOS

Real Mexican *chorizos* are practically impossible to find except in the areas of the United States where there is a large Mexican-American population. They are dark red or reddish brown and sold in links about 3½ inches long. Traditionally they are made of fresh, coarsely ground pork mildly seasoned with paprika, mild chilies, vinegar, herbs, and spices. (The so-called *chorizos*, found in West Coast restaurants, of finely ground beef seasoned with ordinary chili powder and packed in a plastic skin should be avoided—when cooked they resemble a rather messy stew.) You can substitute mild Spanish *chorizos*, which are very widely available. They are generally made of roughly chopped smoked pork seasoned with paprika and other spices, and are therefore more strongly flavored than the Mexican *chorizos*. Since the quality varies enormously, shop around for the best buy. Some brands will keep for weeks under refrigeration.

To cook *chorizos*, remove the skin, and cut or crumble them into small pieces. Fry them slowly until the fat renders out, then brown slightly over a low flame—the spices burn very quickly.

COOKING OIL AND FATS

Although it is generally accepted that good food comes only from good ingredients, so often the quality of cooking oils and fats is overlooked. I always recommend peanut or safflower for these recipes, but even these have a certain raw flavor that is noticeable in the prepared dishes unless the oil is brought up to smoking point—and then the temperature reduced a little—before the *enchiladas*, *tacos*, and so on are fried.

If you can bear to use lard where indicated (it is listed as first preference in the recipes), it gives a very special flavor and consistency to *masa* doughs in particular. Again, look for good quality—possibly a locally made one with a good, rich smell to it and slightly softer than the deathly white lards that are widely distributed and that are made fluffy with stabilizers supposed to make them last a lifetime. Small Italian and Hungarian butcher shops are usually a good source of supply.

CORIANDER

——◦•◦——

Obtaining fresh coriander should not be a problem these days: it is widely available in Mexican, Oriental, and Caribbean markets and in any large supermarkets in such areas as the Southwest, Washington, D. C., and Chicago. You can buy it in fairly large quantities if necessary and keep it for up to three weeks with proper care. If possible, only buy coriander that has the roots attached. Remove all the yellowing leaves, and if it is limp, revive it by immersing it completely in cold water for an hour or so. Place it in an upright container of cold water and cover the leaves with a plastic bag that is held down securely with a rubber band and store in the refrigerator. Renew the water every few days, and remove any deteriorating leaves.

Coriander is called *cilantro* in Mexico and *cilantrillo* in the Caribbean stores. The dried coriander seed will *not* serve in its place, and if you can't get it, leave it out altogether. It does not freeze well whole, but you could, of course, blend it with a little water and freeze in small containers ready to flavor sauces.

Coriander

EPAZOTE

——◦•◦——

Epazote (*Chenopodium ambrosioides*) is *the* Mexican herb *par excellence*. It is a native of tropical America that has spread north, and it can be found growing wild practically all over the United States. I have gathered it in parking lots in Texas cities; along the sidewalks of Richmond, Virginia; in woods in southern Georgia; and in New York's Riverside and Central parks. It is not quite as strong as that grown in Mexico, but it serves very well, particularly in the fall, when it develops its true pungent quality.

You can harvest it in late fall—it is practically the last plant to disappear after the first frosts—and dry it successfully, or you can do what I do: uproot and replant indoors where it will survive the winter. There will always be a few fresh leaves to use, and you have about six weeks' head start in the spring. Or, if you are a true *aficionado*, you will dry the tiny seeds that form on the spikes of the stems and plant them in the spring.

Epazote is commonly known here as "wormseed," or "Mexican tea." There is *no* substitute.

For most Mexicans, it would be unthinkable to cook black beans without a sprig of *epazote* to flavor them. It is said to reduce the gassy effect associated with beans.

A sprig of *epazote*

HERBS

———◆•◆———

Dried herbs will be perfectly adequate for the dishes included here, providing they are whole leaves and not powdered. Oregano, thyme, and bay leaf are the herbs called for in these recipes.

LETTUCE

———◆•◆———

Lettuce is used in abundance in the Mexican kitchen, and the stands in the marketplaces are full of *orejona* (literally "big ear"), romaine lettuces. It is not typically used as a separate salad but as a garnish to be eaten with the food, hot or cold, that it embellishes. The elegant little inner leaves are used whole to decorate an individual plate or serving dish; the larger leaves are shredded finely, and sometimes seasoned with a light dressing, served on top of or around snacks like *tostadas*, *tacos*, and *enchiladas*. *Pozole*, the hearty pork and corn broth of Jalisco, is not complete without a handful of shredded lettuce thrown into the bowl as it is being served. Green sauces—for *enchiladas* or for green *mole*—often call for lettuce leaves to be blended with other ingredients to give color and act as a thickening agent. The insipid iceberg lettuce really won't do.

Here is a simple dressing for the lettuce garnish. Since it should just provide an accent, use sparingly and make it with an ordinary salad oil, not olive oil. Soy oil, for instance, is delicious.

Simple Salad Dressing

⅓ cup salad oil
3 tablespoons wine
vinegar, red or white
½ teaspoon salt
½ teaspoon granulated
sugar
1½ teaspoons prepared
mustard
1 small clove garlic,
peeled and crushed

Mix the ingredients together well and let them season for an hour or so.

MEXICAN GREEN TOMATOES

Mexican green tomatoes are not just unripe ordinary tomatoes, but a member of the *physalis* family—along with the ground cherry and Cape gooseberry—and are covered with a papery green husk. They are known as *fresadillas, tomates verdes,* or *tomatillos,* depending on what part of the country you are in. They are available fresh in many parts of the United States.

To use them for sauces, remove the husk, rinse them briefly in cold water, cover them with water, and simmer them until they are quite soft but not bursting open. This will take about 15 to 20 minutes, depending on their size. If you have freezer space and want to prepare them ahead ready for use, then cook and store them frozen, in their cooking liquid, in one- or two-cup containers.

Where fresh ones are not available, canned ones may be used. There are several brands on the market, some canned in the West and some from Mexico. Of the ones I have tried, without doubt the best value are those with the Clemente Jacques label. The canning liquid is not oversalted and overacidy—which is my chief complaint about the others—for these qualities can ruin any sauce. When using canned *tomates verdes,* drain them, then put them in the blender and blend, along with ⅓ cup water and a pinch of sugar for every cupful of them.

Mexican green husk tomato

PEANUTS

Some of the recipes call for peanuts, which are quite often used in Mexico as a thickening agent in sauces. Ordinary roasted, unsalted nuts should be used. If they are to be fried, heat 1 tablespoon of peanut or safflower oil until smoking, then lower the flame and fry the peanuts, stirring them all the time, until they are a rich, golden brown. It will only take about 2 minutes.

RADISHES

———— ◆◆ ————

Thinly sliced radishes are often used to garnish Mexican snacks, and radish flowers for decorating a dish. To make the flowers, cut four vertical incisions right through the radish from the bulbous top to the stalk base. Then with a very sharp, pointed paring knife cut the red skin as thinly as you can away from the white flesh at the top right down to the base. Cover with cold water and leaves for several hours in the refrigerator. They should open up like flowers.

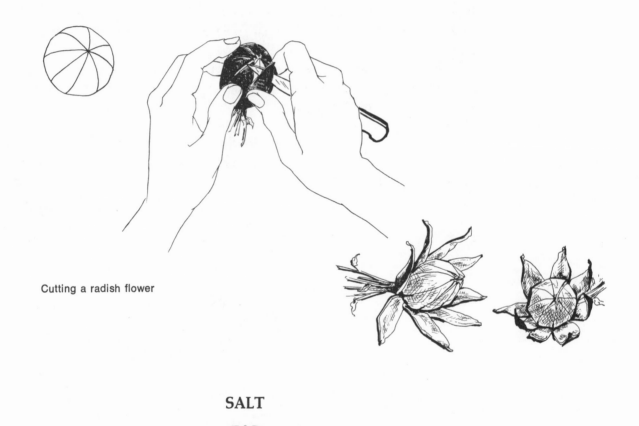

Cutting a radish flower

SALT

———— ◆◆ ————

I would like to recommend that, if you do not already do so, you start using sea or rock salt. You need to use less, and I think food flavors are greatly enhanced thereby. The very hard crystals can be ground down to a powder quickly in any blender, and you don't have to invest in salt mills, which—with the exception of the large Peugeot, which is hard to come by in the United States—I have found to be inefficient or break easily. I do not recommend kosher salt.

SESAME SEEDS

————•◦•————

Some recipes call for toasted sesame seeds. Buy the raw white ones and put them into a small, ungreased frying pan over a medium flame. Keep shaking them gently, or turning them with a spoon, so that they cook evenly. They will begin to look very shiny as the oil comes out of them, and then start to brown. They should be a rich golden color. Watch them constantly, as they will burn very quickly. The whole process will only take about 2 to 3 minutes.

SOUR CREAM

————•◦•————

There are many dishes in the Mexican kitchen that call for cream. The cream used there, especially in the country, is rather thick and slightly acidy. The best substitute, of course, is to make your own, especially for adding to sauces and casseroles that have to be heated—commercial sour cream always gives that "curdled" effect.

Glass jar
½ **pint whipping cream**
2 **tablespoons butter-milk or 1 tablespoon commercial sour cream**

Mix well together in the glass jar and set near a pilot light or warm spot on the stove to thicken. Transfer to the refrigerator for at least 8 hours to thicken further.

The first thickening can take from 6 to 8 hours, depending on many factors. Do not try and hurry it up by putting it in a too-warm place, or a thick skin will form on top and the cream will taste cooked.

There are many tortilla casseroles, snacks, and soups that call for a little sour cream as a final touch just before serving, and this thinned version, which I shall call "prepared sour cream," is perfectly adequate.

Prepared Sour Cream

A blender
2 **cups commercial sour cream**
⅓ **cup milk**
1 **teaspoon salt**

Blend the ingredients together. If left in the refrigerator, the mixture will stabilize and become a little thicker. It will keep perfectly well for several days.

SPICES

Always use whole spices, and grind your own. A mortar and pestle is best for small quantities, and a Moulinex coffee/spice grinder for larger quantities. Whole cumin seeds, peppercorns, cloves, and cinnamon bark are called for in these recipes. Buy the thicker, softer, more fragrant Ceylon cinnamon; it is lighter in color and easier to grind.

TOMATOES

Many authentic Mexican sauces are made with broiled, fresh tomatoes which give the sauces an incomparable flavor and texture. In many places good-quality fresh tomatoes should not be too difficult to obtain the year round. Certainly in New York, where I live and cook for the better part of nine months each year, I cannot remember a day when I haven't been able to find good, overripe tomatoes at bargain prices for my Mexican sauces. If you have good freezer space, you can buy them while they are cheap in the fall, broil, blend, and freeze them ready for use.

If you have to use canned ones, then choose them with care. Try several brands and settle only for those that do not have strong, oversweet, or acidy canning liquids or extra flavorings like basil or oregano. In any case, drain the tomatoes before using them. Never use commercially prepared tomato sauces or purees.

Cooking Methods

FRYING WITH OIL

As I have said elsewhere, it is preferable to bring fresh frying oil up to smoking point before you lower the flame and actually fry food in it. This removes the rather distinctive flavor that most oils have.

Oil that has been used for frying can be used over again, provided it is strained and refrigerated after use.

BROILING TOMATOES FOR SAUCES

Choose tomatoes of equal size so that they will all cook in the same amount of time. Place them on a shallow pan (not too large, or the juice will evaporate and burn) and cook them under a preheated broiler—preferably on medium heat or several inches from the flame so that they do not burn. Turn the tomatoes from time to time so that they cook all the way through. A medium-sized tomato should take about 20 minutes. When they are ready, they should be mushy and the skin blistered and brown.

To use broiled tomatoes for sauces, remove any badly charred pieces of skin and blend the tomatoes with any juices in the pan—skin, core, and everything.

PREPARING DRIED CHILIES

For almost all the recipes in this book using dried chilies, the instructions will read: "toast, clean, and soak the chilies." Here's how you do it.

Heat a griddle or frying pan over a medium flame. Toast the dried chilies lightly, turning them around from time to time—it should take about 4 minutes. Watch the heat and don't let the chilies blister and burn, or the sauce made from them will tend to be bitter. Slit the chilies open and remove the veins and seeds, then cover them with hot water and leave them to soak for about 20 minutes.

Use gloves to clean the chilies if you have particularly sensitive skin, and in any case, after handling them wash your hands well in soapy water and scrub well under the nails. If you don't, you may find your fingertips burning for several hours.

SKINNING FRESH CHILIES AND PREPARING CHILI STRIPS

Put *poblanos* or Anaheim chilies right onto the flame of a gas burner or under a broiler, turning them almost constantly, so that they blister and burn slightly all over. Place them in a plastic bag or damp cloth and let them rest for about 15 minutes. (The skin would actually come off in a very short time, but you want the steam that they generate in the bag to cook the flesh just a little bit.) It is advisable not to do them in the oven, for even when turned to maximum heat, the oven is not fast enough, and the flesh of the chilies will become too mushy. Besides, the charring enhances the flavor of the chili.

The most practical way to clean the chilies is to put a strainer into the sink, under the faucet, then wash the blackened skins off under the running water. (Don't bother, of course, about the strainer if you have a waste disposer.) If you have sensitive skin, wear gloves. Cut the stalk and its base off the chilies and remove all the seeds and veins, which are the hottest part. Chilies vary in strength. If they appear to be very *picante*, leave them to soak in salted water for an hour or so. If you don't wear gloves, try and remember not to rub your eyes or touch your skin until you have scrubbed your hands, especially under the nails, in very soapy water.

Cut the chili flesh in strips roughly about 2 inches by ½ inch.

The Tortilla Vendor

He who sells . . . tortillas, sells thick ones and thin ones. Some are round, some long, some rolled up and round. Some are filled with cooked or uncooked bean paste and are fluffy, and some are filled with chile or meat. There are folded-over tortillas, those that are covered with chile and rolled into balls between the hands, those that are rolled and covered with *chilmole*, and yellow ones and white ones.

He also sells large, thin tortillas and large, thick ones; tortillas made with eggs; those in which the dough is mixed with honey, which are shaped like gloves; small Toluca breads (tortillas)*; tortillas cooked in the coals; tortillas made of amaranth seeds and of ground squash seeds and of green corn and of prickly pears. Some of these are cooked, others toasted; some are cold, others hot.

—Fray Bernardino de Sahagún, *Historia General de las Cosas de Nueva España, Book X, Chapter XVIII* (translated by Thelma Sullivan)

* *He may mean tortillas made from corn that came from Toluca which he mentions in a previous chapter in discussing the corn vendor: "Each variety of corn he sells separately: . . . the corn from Toluca and that of other regions . . ." (Book X, Chapter XVIII, p. 136.)*

Tortillas

The recipes in this book have been test cooked with a standard 5½″ corn (not wheat-flour) tortilla. Some recommendations for the tortillas to be used in the recipes:

Canned tortillas are possibly the most widely distributed, but I cannot recommend them for the recipes in this book.

Frozen and packaged tortillas have a very wide distribution, and can be used for practically all the recipes given here. I do, however, quarrel with the heating instructions on the bag. Try this method:

Open the package and start the defrosting process. As soon as you can do so without tearing them—about 30 minutes—separate them. Heat up some water in a steamer and steam them, two or three at a time, for a few seconds on each side, or until they are thoroughly heated through and flexible. But do not leave them too long or they will become too soft and will probably tear as you lift them out of the steamer.

If you do not have a steamer, improvise. Look for a large, round strainer that just fits snugly into a deep pan, so that there is room for several inches of water in the bottom. The water should come up to just below the strainer; it shouldn't touch it or boil up into it.

Fresh tortillas are being made in enormous quantities not only in the Southwest but all over the country. The quality varies enormously, and really good, light-colored, mealy ones are very difficult to find. So often they are too thin and inclined to be rubbery. In the South I have seen them—and they are in demand—a horrid yellow color. And on my last visit to Mexico City this summer, I was sadly disillusioned to see the quality of most commercial tortillas. They were an unappetizing deep yellow and tasteless: a poor comparison with those whitish, fragrant ones of just a few years ago.

If you really enjoy good food and have a certain amount of patience, why not make your own, at least for a few of the dishes that call for first-class ones?

MASA HARINA—If you want to make your own tortillas and do not have good, fresh *masa* available, then use Quaker *masa harina*, which is widely distributed throughout the United States (call your local Quaker distributor if you cannot find it). It is, as its name implies, especially produced for making tortillas—that is, ground parched corn treated with lime in the traditional manner. Cornmeal and other corn products *simply will not work and cannot be substituted*. When water is added to the flour and the dough has been left to stand for a short period, it proves a quite acceptable substitute for the traditional *masa*. Tortillas made from *masa harina* do, however, tend to be slightly tougher, and do not have such a fine corn flavor.

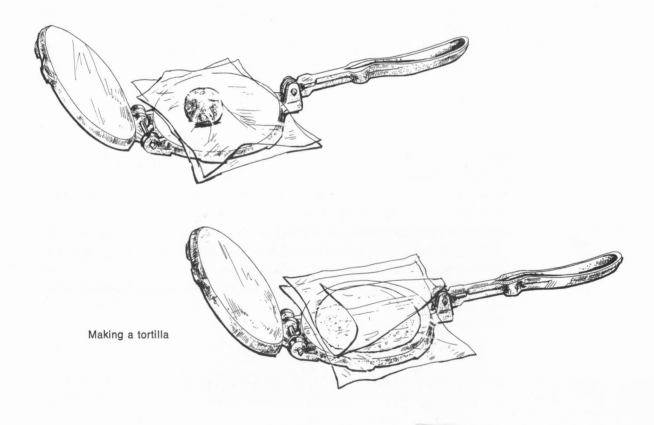

Making a tortilla

Tortillas

16 SMALL TORTILLAS ABOUT 5 INCHES ACROSS

1 or 2 thick griddles or frying pans

1⅓ cups cold water (approximately)
2 cups Quaker *masa harina* or 1½ pounds prepared *masa* (see note below)

A tortilla press
2 sandwich-sized polyethylene bags

Set the pans (it is quicker to work with two) over a medium flame and let them heat up thoroughly; the dough should just sizzle faintly as it touches the pan. Lightly grease the pans before you start making the tortillas.

Add the water all at once to the flour and mix quickly and lightly. Don't compress the dough into hard pieces. Set the dough aside for about 20 minutes, then try it for consistency by making a tortilla.

Open up the tortilla press. Place one of the polyethylene bags on the bottom plate. Take a piece of the tortilla dough and roll it into a ball about 1½ inches across. Flatten the ball slightly and set it onto the bag, a little more toward the hinge than the handle of the press, then place the second bag, flat and smooth, onto the dough. Close the press and push the handle down hard. Open it up and peel off the top bag. Lift the second bag with the flattened tortilla on it, and place, dough side down, on your hand, right or left, more on the fingers than the palm. Peel the bag from the dough—don't attempt to peel the dough from the bag—and lay the tortilla carefully onto the hot griddle. Don't slam it down, or you will get air bubbles in the dough.

Pause at this stage and consider the dough. If the tortilla is rather thick, with a grainy edge, then the dough is too dry. Work a little more water into it. Be careful not to add too much water, or the dough will become unmanageable—it will be impossible to peel the bag off, leaving the dough in one piece—or even if it isn't quite as bad as that, your tortillas will be sodden and won't rise nicely.

If the griddles are at the right heat, the tortilla should take no more than 2 minutes to cook.

Assuming that the dough is now the right consistency, press out the next tortilla and place it on the griddle. When it has just begun to dry out around the edges (don't wait for the dough to dry out completely and curl up, or your tortilla will be tough), flip it over and cook for a slightly longer time on the second side, or until it just begins to color. Flip it back onto the first side and finish cooking through. If the dough is right and the heat of the pans is right, the tortilla should puff up invitingly. (This is the "face" of the tortilla, and this is the side the filling goes on when you are making *tacos* or *enchiladas*.) Remove it from the griddle and keep warm in a thick napkin. As each tortilla is cooked, stack one on top of the other in the napkin and cover. In this way they will retain their heat and flexibility.

As you work, the dough may dry out a little, and you may have to add a little more water.

Almost without exception, where fresh tortillas are available prepared tortilla *masa* is also sold. I have indicated where this could be used—that is, in some of the recipes in the Masa Fantasies chapter (pages 98-113), where the flavor and quality would be greatly enhanced by its use.

In answer to the inevitable question, any masa left over can be frozen, but it tends to make very heavy tortillas. It is better to use it all up while it is fresh and then keep the extra tortillas for such things as *chilaquiles*.

The first few batches may be rather trying (they were to me the first time I made them in New York after living in Mexico, where for many years I had a patient little person in the kitchen patting them out fresh for every meal), but you will soon get the knack of it. Besides, it is the sort of thing the whole family can become involved in.

You can make tortillas about 2 hours ahead of time. Wrap the package of tortillas in foil and reheat in a 275 degree oven before serving.

Totopos or Tostaditas

3 DOZEN

I suppose most people would think of these as "fritos"; in Mexico they are known as *totopos* or *tostaditas*. My first sight of them was when they were stuck around a refried bean roll, giving it a porcupine effect. In fact, they made effective and tasty little scoops with which to eat the mashed beans.

6 dry tortillas

Before they dry out too much, cut the tortillas into six triangular pieces, thus:

A frying pan
Peanut or safflower oil to the depth of ½ inch
Paper toweling

Heat the oil to smoking point in the frying pan, add the tortilla pieces, a few at a time, and fry until they are quite crisp and golden brown. Keep turning them over so that they fry evenly. Drain well and serve.

You can, of course, make these with fresh tortillas, but they will absorb much more of the fat and take longer to cook. Since this is a way of utilizing stale tortillas, and salt is never put into the everyday tortilla dough, if you want them salted, either sprinkle them as they come hot out of the pan or use this more effective, if messy method. Have a bowl of very salty water by the frying pan. Dip a small handful of the tortilla pieces into the water quickly and throw them into the pan—there is a lot of splatter—and fry them crisp.

As long as they are really crisp fried, they can be stored ready for use in an airtight package, but they should be refrigerated or they will become rancid.

Sauces, Garnishes, and Relishes

Cooked Tomato Sauce

1 CUP (ENOUGH FOR 12 TACOS)

This is a very simple and delicious sauce to serve with *tacos*. It is very much better, of course, if made with fresh tomatoes. If you are not serving pickled chilies with the tacos and want a *picante* sauce, then blend 2 fresh *chiles serranos* with the tomatoes. The sauce will freeze.

A blender
  2 medium tomatoes (¾ pound) broiled (page 29), or 1½ cups canned
  ¼ medium onion
  1 clove garlic, peeled
  ¼ teaspoon salt

Blend the ingredients together until smooth.

1½ tablespoons peanut or safflower oil

Heat the oil and cook the puree over a high flame for 3 minutes, stirring almost all the time. Season and keep warm.

Fresh Table Sauce

ABOUT 1½ CUPS

This could almost be considered a national condiment, for it is always there on the Mexican table—the mixture differing slightly in some regions—crisp and refreshing to eat with tortillas alone, *tacos*, eggs, or broiled meats.

1 medium tomato, skin left on ½ medium onion 6 sprigs coriander, leaves only 3 *chiles serranos*, or any small, hot, green chili	Chop the ingredients finely.
½ teaspoon salt, or to taste ⅓ cup cold water	Mix them together with the salt and water and leave to season for about half an hour before serving.

This sauce is best eaten the same day, because it soon loses its crispness and its flavor.

Mexican Green Tomato Sauce

ABOUT 2 CUPS

A blender 1½ cups cooked Mexican green tomatoes plus ½ cup cooking liquid (page 25) *or* 1½ cups canned, drained and then blended with ½ cup water and a pinch of sugar 2 or 3 *chiles serranos* 6 coriander sprigs, leaves only ½ teaspoon salt 1 clove garlic, peeled ¼ medium onion	Blend all the ingredients together for a few seconds, until well amalgamated but not *over*-blended to a smooth froth. Serve at room temperature with a little more chopped coriander sprinkled on top, if desired.

The sauce will keep satisfactorily for a few days, although the fresh coriander flavor will be a little dulled. It does not freeze well. After standing for an hour or so, the sauce will become thick and jelly-like. It can be diluted with a little water or more of the cooking liquid.

Uncooked Tomato Sauce

ABOUT 1½ CUPS

This sauce, with very slight regional variations, is used a great deal in central, northern and western Mexico to garnish *tostadas*, *sopes*, and *tacos*. The original recipe does not have chilies in it, but if you wish to have a *picante* sauce, then broil 3 *chiles serranos* with the tomatoes and blend them together.

There is really no substitute for broiled fresh tomatoes in this case. The sauce is served at room temperature.

A blender	Blend the tomatoes briefly: do not overblend.
3 medium tomatoes (about 14 ounces), broiled (page 29)	
1½ teaspoons vinegar ½ teaspoon salt, or to taste ½ teaspoon dried oregano ⅓ onion, finely chopped	Add the remaining ingredients and leave the sauce to season for at least half an hour before using.

This sauce does not freeze successfully.

Guacamole

Using one average-sized avocado, this recipe should make about 1 to 1¼ cups *guacamole*. It should be made, if possible, just before using. If you have to make it an hour or so ahead, then pack it well into a narrow container and cover tightly with polyethylene wrap to exclude the air.

2 *chiles serranos,* or any small, hot, fresh green chili 3 large coriander sprigs, leaves only ¼ medium onion A mixing bowl	Chop all the ingredients together very finely and put them into the mixing bowl.
1 medium tomato, skin left on	Cut the tomato into very small pieces and add to the rest of the ingredients.
1 medium avocado A small wooden spoon ¼ teaspoon salt, or to taste	Cut the avocado in half, remove the pit, and scoop out the flesh with the wooden spoon. Mash it roughly into the rest of the ingredients. Season and serve.

Carrots and Potatoes

ENOUGH TO GARNISH 12 ENCHILADAS OR TOSTADAS

A saucepan 3 small red bliss or other waxy potatoes (½ pound) 3 medium carrots (½ pound) ¾ teaspoon salt Boiling water to cover ¼ cup white vinegar	Peel the potatoes—or the skins can be left on—scrape the carrots and cut into ½-inch dice. Put into the pan with the salt and barely cover with boiling water, then bring to a boil and cook very quickly for 4 minutes. Remove from the flame, add the vinegar to the water, and set aside for at least 30 minutes. Drain well and use as a garnish.

The vegetables should remain slightly crisp.

Pickled Onion Rings

ENOUGH TO GARNISH 12 TOSTADAS

A large colander
2 medium onions,
    white or purple
Boiling water to cover
A glass or china bowl
½ cup white vinegar
½ cup cold water
1 teaspoon salt

Slice the onions into thin rings. Spread them out in the colander and pour the boiling water over them.

Turn into the china or glass bowl; add the rest of the ingredients and let soak for at least 30 minutes, turning them over from time to time.

Best used fresh, but can be kept in the refrigerator for a few days, although they will lose their crispness.

Easy Snacks

GENERAL NOTES ON TOSTADAS

One of the simplest snacks of all in Mexico is the *tostada*, a tortilla that has been fried almost crisp and piled high with lots of shredded meat, lettuce, cheese, or whatever you have around.

1. It is not necessary, nor indeed advisable, to use freshly made tortillas for *tostadas*. It is better if they are made several hours ahead, so that they will not absorb too much oil. Or you can use defrosted tortillas perfectly well.

2. Only fry as many tortillas as you can accommodate comfortably in your frying pan—they should lie flat in the frying oil and not overlap. If they start to curl up as they cook, then flatten them with a metal spatula.

3. Correctly cooked, the tostadas should be crisp around the edge and golden brown but not hard toward the center. If they are too crisp throughout they will tend to break at first bite and you will be left with a handful of *guacamole*, or whatever the topping may be. I always think of it as an edible plate. No use trying to take a knife and fork to tostadas; they are "finger food"—although you will probably need both hands.

Names always get changed somewhere along the line and, of course, in parts of northern Mexico and along the border they are confusingly called *chalupas* (see page 47).

Guacamole and Sour Cream Tostadas

6 SERVINGS

Have ready:

12 tortillas
 2 cups Guacamole (see page 42)
 1 cup Prepared Sour Cream (see page 27)
1½ cups shredded and dressed lettuce (see page 24)
4 to 6 canned *chiles jalapeños*, cut into strips

A frying pan Peanut or safflower oil to a depth of ½ inch The tortillas Paper toweling	Heat the oil and fry the tortillas until crisp around the edge, but not too hard. Drain well.

½ pound mild
    Cheddar, Muenster,
    or jack cheese
The garnish (see above)
	Cut the cheese into thin slices; put them on the tortillas and melt under a broiler or in the oven. Garnish each *tostada* with a large spoonful of the *guacamole*, a little sour cream, some shredded lettuce, and some chili strips. Serve immediately.

In Mexico *queso Chihuahua* would be used.

Pig's Feet Tostadas (*from San Luis Potosí*)

6 SERVINGS

Have ready:

12 tortillas, cold or defrosted
1½ cups finely shredded and dressed lettuce (see page 24)
1 small avocado, sliced (see page 16)
1½ cups Uncooked Tomato Sauce (see page 41)
3 tablespoons finely grated Sardo cheese
1 medium onion, preferably purple, thinly sliced

A saucepan
  2 fresh pig's feet, split in half
  1 small bay leaf
  ⅛ teaspoon dried thyme
  ¼ teaspoon dried oregano
  2 cloves garlic, peeled
  ½ medium onion, sliced
  6 peppercorns
  1 tablespoon salt, or to taste

Put all the ingredients into the saucepan and cover with cold water ½ inch above the level of the ingredients. Bring slowly to a boil, then lower the flame and simmer for about 2½ hours. (The meat should be tender but not too soft.) Set aside to cool in the broth.

When the pig's feet are cool enough to handle, remove all the bones carefully and chop the meat, gelatinous gristle, and rind into small pieces.

A shallow dish
  (8 × 8 × 2)
Freshly ground pepper
Salt as necessary

Place the meat in the shallow dish and season with salt and pepper (bearing in mind that cooked foods served cold need to be more highly seasoned).

The strained broth

Strain the broth and pour 1⅓ cups of it over the meat. Set the dish in the refrigerator until firmly set—about 1 hour.

A frying pan
Peanut or safflower oil to a depth of ½ inch
The tortillas
Paper toweling

Heat the oil and fry the tortillas until crisp around the edge but not too hard. Drain well.

The pig's feet jelly
The garnish (see above)

Cut the pig's feet jelly into small squares and put 2 to 3 heaped tablespoons onto each *tostada*. Cover with lettuce, some slices of avocado, sauce, cheese, and last of all the onion rings.

Any jellied pig's feet left over can be used as it is for an appetizer, served with lemon quarters and plenty of finely chopped parsley.

The tendency generally is to overcook pig's feet, so that the flesh becomes too soft and insipid. They vary considerably in size, so cooking time may have to be adjusted. Try and choose ones that are between ¾ and 1 pound each. I quite often err on time and undercook to try and get the right consistency, sometimes forgetting that, soft as they may be hot, they stiffen up considerably as they cool down.

Nuevo León Chalupas

6 SERVINGS

The word *chalupa* means "little boat," and in most of Mexico boat-shaped pieces of tortilla dough are cooked, pinched up at the edge, garnished with chili sauce, shredded meat, and what you will, and served as *chalupas*. But in Nuevo León, for some reason, the garnished fried tortilla (*tostada*) has come to be called *chalupa*.

Have ready:

12 tortillas, cold or defrosted
 2 cups Refried Pinto Beans (see page 18)
6 to 8 ounces Cheddar, Muenster, or jack cheese, thinly sliced
 1 large avocado, sliced and dressed (see page 16)

A frying pan **Peanut or safflower oil to a depth of ¼ inch** **The tortillas** **Paper toweling**	Heat the oil and fry the tortillas, a few at a time, until crisp around the edge but not too hard. Drain well.
The bean paste **The sliced cheese**	Spread about 2 spoonfuls of the bean paste over each tortilla. Put some slices of cheese over the paste, then place the tostadas under a hot broiler or in the oven until the cheese just begins to melt.
The sliced avocado	Garnish with the avocado slices and serve.

In Mexico *queso Chihuahua* would be used.

Exquisite Tortillas

6 SERVINGS

The Mexican's delicious answer to the American ham and cheese sandwich.

Have ready:

     12 tortillas, cold or defrosted
     ¾ cup Prepared Sour Cream (see page 27)
     ¾ cup Mexican Green Tomato Sauce (see page 40), Guacamole (see page 42) or Uncooked Tomato Sauce (see page 41)
     1 small onion, finely chopped
    1½ cups shredded lettuce, lightly dressed with oil and vinegar
     6 radishes, cut into flowers (see page 26) or sliced

The tortillas
    6 ounces cooked ham, thinly sliced
    6 ounces mild Cheddar, Meunster, or jack cheese, finely sliced
Toothpicks

Lay 6 of the tortillas out flat; spread each one with some of the ham and cheese. Cover each with another tortilla, to form a sandwich, then secure each pair of tortillas together with 2 toothpicks, one on each side.

A frying pan
Peanut or safflower oil to a depth of ¼ inch
Paper toweling
The garnish (see above)

Heat the oil and fry each sandwich on either side until just beginning to get crisp, not hard. Drain well, then garnish with the sour cream, sauce, and chopped onion. Decorate each plate with the lettuce and radishes, which will also serve as a foil for the richness of the tortillas.

These will hold, in a 375-degree oven, for a short time only. Beyond that the cheese will harden, and if the oven is lower, the tortillas will go leathery.

In Mexico *queso Chihuahua* would be used.

Chiles Capones (*with chiles poblanos*)

6 SERVINGS

I was a bit doubtful about recommending this recipe until I tried it recently with small *chiles poblanos* that I had brought back with me from the West Coast. *Muy mexicano! Muy ranchero!*—especially for those who like peasant and earthy food. I had remembered trying something like it in Mexico City, but was unimpressed: the tortilla was of wheat flour and there was no fragrant *epazote* in the cheese filling. Make them only if you have fresh *poblanos* and *epazote* at hand. The long, green Californian chilies do not have such a rich flavor, and the canned ones will simply not do in this recipe. You will need about ¼ pound of butter and ⅓ cup oil to fry the 12 tortillas.

A bowl
  2 cups well-salted farmer cheese
½ cup finely chopped *epazote* leaves, approximately
Salt, if necessary

Mix the cheese, *epazote* leaves, and salt well together.

12 small, whole *chiles poblanos*, peeled and cleaned (see page 30)

Stuff about 2 tablespoons of the cheese mixture into each chili.

A frying pan
Melted butter and oil, mixed, to a depth of ¼ inch, more if necessary
12 tortillas
Paper toweling
The stuffed chilies

Heat the fat and fry the chilies for about 5 minutes. Remove, and in the same fat, fry the tortillas briefly on both sides. Drain well, then wrap a tortilla around each of the chilies. Serve immediately.

In Mexico *queso fresco* would be used.

Mexican Scrambled Eggs with Totopos

4 SERVINGS

A frying pan
Peanut or safflower oil to
    a depth of ¼ inch
 6 dry tortillas, cut into
    6 pieces, thus:
Paper toweling

Heat the oil and fry the tortilla pieces, one half at a time, so they cook evenly. They should be just a little hard but not browned. Drain and keep warm.

½ medium onion
 1 large tomato (½
    pound), skin left on,
    or 1 cup canned,
    drained
4 to 6 *chiles serranos*
A frying pan
¼ cup peanut or
    safflower oil

Chop all the ingredients finely. Heat the oil, then add the chopped ingredients to the pan and cook over a medium flame for 5 minutes, stirring the mixture from time to time.

A mixing bowl
An egg beater
 6 large eggs (16 ounces
    by weight)
½ teaspoon salt
The *totopos*

Beat the eggs together with the salt and add them, with the totopos, to the pan. Cook, stirring, until the eggs are set but not too dry.

This makes a very good brunch dish.

"Tortilla Soup"

4 TO 6 SERVINGS

This was called simply "tortilla soup" in the book where I found this recipe—what an understatement! It is in fact a fanciful and colorful concoction of fried tortillas stacked with *guacamole*, sour cream, and cheese and smothered in tomato sauce.

Have ready:

 12 tortillas, freshly made, if possible, and not too thin
A warmed serving dish just large enough to accommodate 3 tortillas laid flat
1½ cups Guacamole (see page 42)

4 ounces Cheddar cheese, grated, or farmer cheese, crumbled
¾ cup Prepared Sour Cream (see page 27)

A frying pan
  2 tablespoons peanut
    or safflower oil
  5 green onions, finely
    chopped
	Heat the oil and cook the onions gently until they are soft but not browned.

A blender
  1 pound tomatoes,
    peeled and chopped,
    or 2 cups canned,
    drained
  2 cloves garlic, peeled
  ¾ teaspoon salt, or to
    taste
	Blend the tomatoes with the garlic.
	
	Add to the pan with the salt and fry the sauce over a fairly high flame, stirring and scraping the bottom of the pan almost constantly, until it has reduced and seasoned—about 5 minutes. Set aside and keep warm.

A frying pan Peanut or safflower oil to a depth of ¼ inch The tortillas Paper toweling	Heat the oil and fry the tortillas briefly on both sides. Drain well.
The sauce The warmed serving dish The *guacamole* The cheese The sour cream	Dip 3 of the tortillas into the sauce and lay them flat onto the serving dish. Spread them with about 2 tablespoons each of the *guacamole*, a little cheese, and some sour cream. Dip 3 more tortillas into the sauce and cover the filling. Repeat with another layer of tortillas on top of the first "sandwich," then repeat a layer of *guacamole*, cheese, and sour cream, ending with a layer of the remaining tortillas. Pour the rest of the sauce over the stacks of tortillas and sprinkle the remaining cheese over the top. Cut into wedges and serve immediately.

This is quite obviously a dish that has to be prepared at the very last moment. Only the sauce can be done ahead of time. The minute the *guacamole* is made, preparations for the rest should start.

In Mexico *queso fresco* would be used.

Chiles Capones (*with chiles jalapeños*)

6 SERVINGS

Chiles capones can also be prepared with fresh *jalapeños*—for a more fiery version. This is pan-to-mouth food that must be eaten immediately it is ready, and without ceremony.

Have ready:

12 tortillas, freshly made, if possible, and still warm
 1 cup Prepared Sour Cream (see page 27)

A saucepan 12 large, fresh *chiles jalapeños*, peeled as for Anaheim chilies (see page 30), but on a frying pan or griddle instead of the flame	Make an incision down one side of each chili, leaving the top and stalk intact, and carefully scrape out the veins and seeds. Put into a saucepan and cover well with cold water. Add the salt, bring to a boil, and let simmer for 5 minutes. Drain and dry on paper toweling.

A bowl
4 to 6 ounces farmer
     cheese (about ¾ to
     1 cup)
 1 heaped tablespoon
     chopped *epazote*
     leaves
 1 teaspoon salt

Combine the ingredients and use to stuff the chilies.

A frying pan
Peanut or safflower oil to
     a depth of ¼ inch

Heat the oil and place the chilies, open side up, into the pan in one layer. Fry them gently, turning them at intervals slightly to one side and then the other (do not let them cook with the open side down or the filling will melt and run out). This should take about 7 minutes.

The stuffed chilies
The tortillas
The sour cream

Put each chili into a warm tortilla, cover with a little of the cream, fold over, and serve immediately.

Tacos

"... that while Moctezuma was at table eating, as I have described, there were waiting on him two other graceful women to bring him tortillas, kneaded with eggs and other sustaining ingredients, and these tortillas were very white and they were brought on plates covered with clean napkins. ..."

The Discovery and Conquest of Mexico 1517–1521
by Bernal Díaz del Castillo

To most people in the United States, a *taco* is a tortilla bent in half to form a deep U shape, then fried crisp and stuffed to overflowing with ground beef, shredded iceberg lettuce, sliced tomato, and grated cheese. Throughout Mexico, however the simple *taco* consumed by millions of people daily is a fresh, hot tortilla rolled around some shredded meat or mashed beans and liberally doused with any one of the endless variety of sauces for which Mexico is justly famed, but which are sadly misrepresented this side of the border. This is great eating if you have a convenient supply of good-quality, fresh tortillas or make your own. But if you have to use indifferent commercial ones—or prefer them fried anyway—it would be better to fry your *tacos*.

53

Tacos are usually eaten as a snack between meals, in the evening with a bowl of soup for supper, or as an appetizer before the main meal of the day. They are a finger food, so don't be stuffy and try to eat them with a knife and fork.

NOTES ON FILLING AND FRYING TACOS

1. Put a little of the prepared filling across—but slightly to one side—on the face of the tortilla (see illustration). Start from that side and roll it up fairly firmly but not too tightly, then secure the edge with a toothpick so that it does not become unrolled. Providing the filling is not too hot so that it will make the tortilla soggy, this can be done ahead of time.

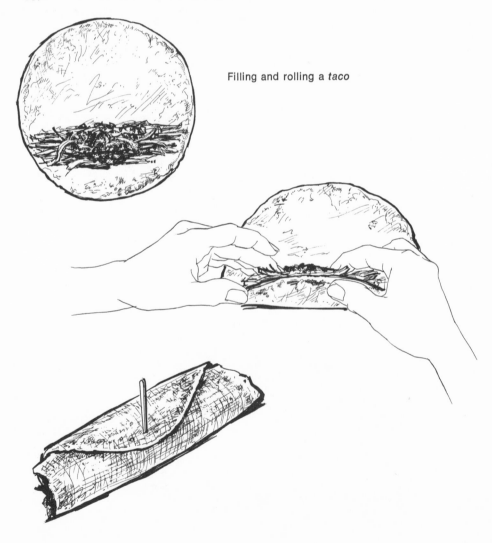

Filling and rolling a *taco*

2. Lard is, of course, ideal for frying *tacos*. It gives the *masa* a distinctive flavor and texture. If you prefer to use oil, then be sure to choose a good quality one, and always bring fresh oil up to the smoking point before attempting to fry in it.

3. There should be no more than ¼ inch of fat in the pan, so that it will not seep into the filling. It should also be very hot for frying, or it will be absorbed by the tortilla.

4. Fry the *taco* for a minute or so with the open edge on top. As it becomes golden underneath—not too hard—then roll it, removing the toothpick, so that the open edge is underneath (you may need to press it down a little at this point to prevent it from opening up). Continue frying until it is slightly crisp and golden all the way around. Drain well on paper toweling and serve immediately.

5. *Tacos* will hold for a very short time only, in a 375-degree oven, before the filling starts to dry up at the ends: if held in a slower oven, they tend to become leathery.

6. Traditionally and generally—there are just a few regional exceptions—Mexicans do not like their *tacos* fried to a crisp. Ideally they should be slightly crisp on the outside and slightly doughy inside, so you can still taste the corn and the texture of the tortilla.

7. If you are using defrosted or rather dry tortillas and they break when you try to roll them, see the note on steaming, page 33.

MEAT FILLING FOR TACOS

In most of Mexico—I can think of a few regional exceptions—the preferred method of preparing meat as a filling for *tacos* and *enchiladas* is to cook and shred it. It may be more trouble, but you can soon learn to do it quickly. It gives a much better texture and flavor than a ground meat filling, and besides, you will have a delicious broth—it can be frozen, if necessary—to use as a base for soups, and for sauces and rice. Pork and chicken are the most popular of the meats prepared this way.

For filling 12 *tacos* you will need about 1⅓ to 1½ cups of shredded meat; for 12 *enchiladas*, from 1½ to 2 cups—depending, of course, on the size of the tortillas used and how extravagant you want to be.

One pound of boneless meat, with some fat for flavor, will yield from 1 to 1⅓ cups meat.

Pork, Cooked and Shredded

A saucepan
 2 pounds boneless pork
Pork bones, if any
¼ medium onion,
    roughly sliced
 1 large clove garlic,
    peeled
Salt to taste
 5 peppercorns

Cut the meat into large cubes, put it into the saucepan with the other ingredients, and cover with cold water. Bring to a boil, then lower the flame and simmer until *just* tender—about 45 minutes. Remove from the flame and let the meat cool off in the broth. When the meat is cool enough to handle, drain, reserving the broth. Shred the meat (see note below) and add more salt as necessary.

Be careful not to overcook the meat, remembering that the cooking process goes on as the meat cools off in the broth.

The meat can either be shredded by hand, with the tines of two forks back to back, or lightly pounded in a mortar just until the fibers separate.

Beef, Cooked and Shredded

If beef is preferred to pork, cook in exactly the same way, but allowing an hour, at least, for the cooking time.

Chicken, Cooked and Shredded

A 3-pound chicken will yield about 2½ cups of cooked and shredded meat (the breast will yield about 1 cup, leg and thigh together ½ cup each, the two wings and extra pickings another ½ cup). About 1½ cups are sufficient for 12 *tacos*, and 1½ to 2 cups for *enchiladas*, which are rolled more loosely. Cover a 3-pound chicken with chicken broth (either homemade or made with two chicken bouillon cubes of good quality). Bring to a boil, then reduce the heat and simmer, breast down, for 20 minutes. Turn the chicken over and simmer for another 20 minutes, then turn off the heat and leave to cool off in the broth. When cool enough to handle, remove the skin and bones and shred the meat (which is easier to do with your fingers, if not with the tines of two forks back to back). Be sure to reserve the broth.

Always season the shredded meat well with more salt and keep it warm, ready to fill the *tacos* or *enchiladas*. If you like to add more flavor, chop some of the skin and add it to the meat. You should choose even bouillon cubes with care: Knorr is about the best that I have come across, but there may be others. Never buy those which are intensely yellow and grossly overseasoned.

Potato Tacos

4 TO 6 SERVINGS

Have ready:

12 tortillas
⅔ cup Sour Cream (see page 27)
 1 cup Cooked Tomato Sauce (see page 39)
1½ cups shredded lettuce
Pickled *chiles jalapeños, largos, bolitos,* or yellow chilies

A bowl
 ¾ pound cooked red
   bliss or other waxy
   potatoes, unpeeled
 ½ medium onion
  4 ounces (¾ cup)
   farmer cheese
 ½ teaspoon salt

Chop the potatoes finely, with their skins, and mix with the rest of the ingredients.

Fill each tortilla with about 2 tablespoons of the mixture and secure with toothpicks.

Heat the oil and fry as for all *taco* recipes (see page 54). Drain well.

The tortillas
A frying pan
Peanut or safflower oil to
   a depth of ¼ inch
Paper toweling
The garnish (see above)

Serve immediately, garnished with the warm sauce, sour cream, and lettuce. Serve the chilies separately.

The original recipe calls for a plain mashed-potato filling. I happen to like potato skins and the texture they give to the filling, and have improvised this, keeping within the Mexican tradition. Surprisingly, the potato and *masa* go very well together, and make a simple and tasty budget dish.

You could even use some chopped *epazote* leaves in the filling.

In Mexico *queso fresco* would be used.

Chorizo and Potato Tacos

4 TO 6 SERVINGS

Have ready:

12 tortillas
 1 cup Mexican Green Tomato Sauce (see page 40)

A frying pan
 3 *chorizos*, each 4
     inches long
 6 small red bliss or
     other waxy potatoes
     (¾ pound), crisp
     cooked and diced
 3 canned *chiles
     chipotles*
 ¼ teaspoon salt, or to
     taste

Skin and crumble the *chorizos* and cook over low heat until the fat begins to render out.

Add the potatoes and chilies with salt to taste and continue cooking until the mixture is well seasoned and the potatoes are beginning to brown (about 8 minutes), stirring well from time to time.

A frying pan
The tortillas
Peanut or safflower oil to
     a depth of ¼ inch
Paper toweling

Fill and fry the *tacos* in the usual way (see page 54), then drain and serve immediately. Hand the sauce separately.

Taquitos

6 SERVINGS

I came across this simple suggestion for *tacos* when I had a refrigerator full of Mexican bits and pieces. There was half a big avocado, a little package of frozen refried beans that kept falling out with the ice trays, and a half-finished can of *chiles chipotles*. You don't have to have these ingredients, but it does make you stop and realize that practically all leftovers can be made up into savory and simple tacos.

12 tortillas
 1 small avocado, cut
     into 12 slices (see
     page 16)
 4 ounces mild Cheddar,
     Muenster, or similar
     cheese, cut into strips

On each tortilla put a slice of avocado, some strips of cheese, a piece or two of chili, a tablespoon of beans, and a thin slice of onion. Sprinkle well with salt, roll the tortillas up, and secure with a toothpick.

4–6 canned *chiles
    chipotles*, each cut
    into 3 pieces
¾ cup refried beans
    (see page 18)
12 thin slices onion
Salt to taste
Toothpicks
A frying pan
Peanut or safflower oil
    to a depth of ¼ inch
Paper toweling
  6 romaine lettuce
    leaves
  6 large radishes, thinly
    sliced
  3 tablespoons roughly
    chopped coriander
    leaves, approxi-
    mately

Fry until golden but not too crisp (see page 54). Drain on paper toweling and serve garnished with the lettuce, radishes, and chopped coriander.

Mexican Scrambled Egg Tacos

4 to 6 servings

½ medium onion
  1 large tomato (½
    pound), skin left on,
    or 1 cup canned,
    drained
4 to 6 *chiles serranos*
A frying pan
¼ cup peanut or saf-
    flower oil

Chop the onion, tomato, and chilies finely. Heat the oil to smoking, then lower flame. Add the chopped ingredients to the pan and cook over a medium flame, stirring the mixture from time to time, for about 5 minutes.

  6 large eggs (16 ounces
    by weight)
½ teaspoon salt
12 tortillas
Paper toweling

Beat the eggs together with the salt and add them to the pan. Stir until the eggs are set but not too dry, then put 2 tablespoons of the mixture into each tortilla, roll up, fasten with toothpicks, and fry (see page 54). Drain and serve immediately.

Sour Cream Tacos

4 TO 6 SERVINGS

The original name for this dish was *taquitos de nata*—in fact the sauce was thickened with *natas*, which are the skimmings from good, rich, unhomogenized milk as it is scalded.

Have ready:

1½ to 2 cups cooked, shredded, and well-salted chicken (see page 56)
12 tortillas
An ovenproof serving dish (ideally 9 × 13½ × 2)
½ medium onion, finely chopped

¾ pound tomatoes, broiled (see page 29), or 1½ cups canned, drained	Blend the tomatoes with the rest of the ingredients.
¼ medium onion	
1 clove garlic, peeled	
¾ teaspoon salt, or to taste	

A frying pan	Heat the oil and fry the shredded chicken for a minute or so over a fairly hot flame, stirring constantly, until it just begins to brown. Add the puree and chili strips and continue cooking and stirring until almost dry. Set aside and keep warm.
2 tablespoons peanut or safflower oil	
The cooked chicken	
¾ cup of the tomato puree	
1 fresh *chile jalapeño* or any fresh, hot green chili, cut into thin strips	

A frying pan	Heat the oil and fry the remainder of the puree over a fairly high flame for about 3 minutes, stirring constantly. Remove from the heat and stir in the sour cream. Set aside and keep warm.
1 tablespoon peanut or safflower oil	
½ cup sour cream, either commercial or homemade (see page 27) at room temperature	

A frying pan	Heat the oil and lightly fry the tortillas, a few
Peanut or safflower oil	at a time, on both sides. Drain well.
to a depth of ¼ inch	
The tortillas	Preheat the oven to 375 degrees.
Paper toweling	
The chicken filling	Put a little of the filling on each of the
The serving dish	tortillas, roll up, and place side by side on the
The sauce	serving dish. Pour the sauce down the center
The finely chopped	of the *tacos* and bake for 10 minutes. Garnish
onion	with the onion and serve immediately.

The tacos should not be left for a longer period in the oven or they will become tough and the sauce will dry out. You could get the filling and sauce made ahead and then assemble and bake at the last moment.

The original recipe did not call for the chili or the onion garnish. They are authentic touches that I think improve this very simple and delicious dish.

The tacos are not completely smothered by the sauce, so the ends are slightly crisp while the center is soft.

Tacos of Chili Strips (*from Zacatecas*)

6 SERVINGS

Have ready:

A warmed serving dish (ideally 9 × 13½ × 2)
12 tortillas
1⅓ cups Prepared Sour Cream (see page 27)

A frying pan
   2 tablespoons peanut
      or vegetable oil
   3 *chiles poblanos,*
      peeled and cleaned
      (see page 30), or 5
      canned, peeled
      green chilies

Heat the oil. Cut the chilies into narrow strips and cook them over a low flame for about 3 minutes (or 1 minute only for canned chilies).

A blender
   ½ pound tomatoes,
      broiled (see page
      29), or 1 cup
      canned, drained
   ⅓ medium onion
   ¾ teaspoon salt, or to
      taste
Freshly ground black
      pepper

Blend the tomatoes with the onion until smooth, then add the puree to the chilies in the pan. Season with salt and pepper and cook over a medium flame for about 5 minutes, stirring and scraping the bottom of the pan almost constantly.

   3 large eggs

Beat the eggs lightly and stir them into the mixture. Continue stirring until they are just set, then remove from the heat and keep warm.

A frying pan
Peanut or safflower oil to
      a depth of ¼ inch
The tortillas
Paper toweling
The filling
The serving dish
The sour cream

Heat the oil and fry the tortillas on both sides. Fry a little more than you would for *enchiladas* (see page 115), but not allowing them to get so crisp that you cannot easily fold them over. Drain well, then fill each one with a little of the chili-egg filling. Double the tortillas over and set on the serving dish.

Pour the sour cream over the *tacos* and serve immediately.

These would hold for a few minutes in a 375-degree oven, but they do get leathery if left much longer.

Tacos de Fortunata (*from Aguascalientes*)

4 TO 6 SERVINGS

Have ready:

12 tortillas
A large serving platter or individual dishes
 2 cups finely shredded lettuce
 6 tablespoons grated Romano cheese
¾ cup Uncooked Tomato Sauce (sèe page 41), made with 3 to 4 *chiles serranos*, Mexican Green Tomato Sauce (see page 40), or Cooked Tomato Sauce (see page 39)

A frying pan
 2 tablespoons peanut or safflower oil
½ medium onion, finely chopped
½ pound lean ground beef
½ pound lean ground pork

Heat the oil and fry the onion until soft but not brown. Add the ground meats and cook over a low flame for about 10 minutes, turning it over from time to time.

A blender
 1 large tomato (10 ounces), broiled (see page 29), or 1 cup canned, drained
 2 small cloves garlic, peeled
Pinch of cumin seeds
 1 teaspoon salt
The tortillas
Toothpicks

Blend the tomato with the garlic and cumin until smooth. Add with salt to the meats in the pan and continue cooking over a fairly high flame until the mixture is almost dry—about 8 minutes.

Put a large spoonful of the mixture into the tortillas, double them over, and secure each with a toothpick.

Peanut or safflower oil or melted lard to a depth of ¼ inch
Paper toweling
The serving platter or dishes
The garnish (see above)

Heat the oil and fry the *tacos* until they are slightly crisp. Drain, then place on the serving platter or dishes and serve on a bed of lettuce, each one topped with a spoonful of sauce and some grated cheese.

(*continued*)

These should be served immediately or they will soon go rather leathery.

In Mexico *queso añejo* would be used, and a sauce of *chile mirasol*.

Any leftover roast meat could be used up in this recipe. It could be chopped up rather coarsely (the original recipe actually calls for it like that, rather than ground meat) and added to the onion with the blended tomato-garlic mixture.

Beef Tacos

4 TO 6 SERVINGS

Have ready:

  12 tortillas
   1 cup Cooked Tomato Sauce (see page 39)
  ¾ cup Prepared Sour Cream (see page 27)
  ½ cup crumbled farmer cheese (about 3 ounces)

A frying pan
1½ tablespoons peanut or safflower oil
½ medium onion, thinly sliced
1 pound cooked and shredded beef (see page 56)

Heat the oil and fry the onion gently until soft but not brown. Add the meat and cook over a medium flame, stirring from time to time, until it is lightly browned. Set aside to cool a little.

The tortillas
Toothpicks
A frying pan
Peanut or safflower oil to a depth of ¼ inch
Paper toweling
The garnish (see above)

Fill the tortillas and fry in the usual way (see page 54). Drain, then serve immediately with the sauce, sour cream, and cheese as a garnish.

This is a good way of using up leftover roast beef. Atypically, I like to add a strip or two of fresh *chile jalapeño* to the meat in the *tacos*.

In Mexico *queso fresco* would be used.

Mushroom Tacos

4 TO 6 SERVINGS

Have ready:

12 tortillas
Prepared Sour Cream (see page 27) (optional)

A frying pan
3 tablespoons peanut or safflower oil
1 small onion, finely chopped
2 cloves garlic, peeled and chopped

Heat the oil and fry the onion and garlic gently for a few seconds; do not let them brown.

2 medium tomatoes (¾ pound), peeled and chopped, or 1½ cups canned, drained
3 *chiles serranos* or any fresh, green chilies
1 teaspoon salt, or to taste
1 pound mushrooms, finely sliced

Add the tomatoes, chilies, salt and mushrooms; cook over a medium flame, uncovered, stirring the mixture from time to time until the mushrooms are soft and the juices reduced—about 20 minutes.

2 sprigs *epazote* or parsley, leaves only, roughly chopped

Add the *epazote* and cook for 1 minute more. Set aside to cool a little.

The tortillas
Toothpicks
A frying pan
Melted lard or peanut or safflower oil to a depth of ¼ inch
Paper toweling
The sour cream

Put a little of the mixture onto each of the tortillas, roll them up, and secure with a toothpick. Heat the fat and fry the *tacos* until they are just crisping but not hard (see page 55). Drain them well and serve them immediately, either plain or with a little prepared sour cream.

These will hold for a short time in a 375-degree oven; beyond that they will begin to dry out. If the oven is at a lower temperature, they will become leathery.

The original recipe calls for the black fungus or smut that grows on the corn, which is delicious. Any wild mushroom could in fact be used.

Tacos from Aguascalientes

4 TO 6 SERVINGS

Have ready:

12 tortillas
A serving dish (ideally 9 × 13½ × 2)
 1 cup well-seasoned cooked and shredded meat (see page 55)
Romaine lettuce leaves
 6 large radishes, thinly sliced
 1 medium onion (purple, if possible), thinly sliced
¼ cup well-salted farmer cheese, crumbled

A blender
 4 *chiles poblanos*, peeled and cleaned (see page 30) or 6 canned, peeled green chilies, seeded
¼ medium onion
 1 clove garlic, peeled

Blend the chilies with the onion and garlic until smooth.

A frying pan
 1 tablespoon peanut or safflower oil

Heat the oil and cook the chili puree over a medium flame for about 3 minutes, stirring it the whole time.

⅔ cup milk
⅔ cup commercial or homemade sour cream (see page 27)
½ teaspoon salt, or to taste

Remove from heat, then add the milk, sour cream, and salt and heat through over a low flame. Set aside and keep warm.

½ pound farmer cheese, sliced
 1 avocado, sliced (see page 16)
Salt to taste
The cooked meat
The tortillas

Put a slice of the cheese, a slice of avocado, some salt, and a little of the meat onto each tortilla. Roll the tortilla up and fasten with a toothpick.

A frying pan
Peanut or safflower oil or melted lard to a depth of ¼ inch

Heat the oil and fry the *tacos* until they are slightly crisp (see notes page 54). Drain well, then place on the serving dish, pour the sauce over, garnish, and serve immediately.

Paper toweling
The serving dish
The garnish (see above)

The sauce can be made ahead and everything prepared and ready to assemble, but once fried the *tacos* must be served immediately.

If you fry in lard, the flavor will be much better.

Any leftover roast meat would do for these *tacos*, and the stronger the seasoning the better. The original recipe calls for shredded barbecued meat, and it is almost certain that the meat would have been dressed with a light chili sauce before being cooked.

In Mexico *queso fresco* would be used.

Soups

"Novices, as a rule, find the warm, damp, flabby tortilla, insipid and unpalateable, but the veterans are as fond of them as the Indians themselves."

From "A Peep at Mexico"
by John Lewis Geiger (1874)

———•◦•———

Tortilla Soup

6 SERVINGS

Have ready:

 6 cups chicken broth
12 tortillas, cut into strips, thus:
 3 *chiles pasillas*, fried and crumbled
 6 heaping tablespoons grated Cheddar cheese

A blender
 2 medium tomatoes,

Blend the tomatoes with the rest of the ingredients.

68

    broiled (see page
    29) or 1½ cups
    canned, drained
⅓ medium onion,
    roughly chopped
1 clove garlic, peeled
    and roughly
    chopped

A frying pan 1 tablespoon peanut or safflower oil **The broth** **Salt as necessary**	Heat the oil and fry the tomato puree over a fairly high flame for about 3 minutes, stirring it all the time. Add the broth, adjust the seasoning, and simmer for about 5 minutes longer. Remove from the heat and keep warm.

A frying pan
Peanut or safflower oil
    to a depth of ½
    inch
The tortilla pieces
Paper toweling
	Heat the oil and fry the tortilla strips, about one third at a time so that they are fried evenly, until they are just beginning to stiffen but are not brown. Drain well.

2 sprigs *epazote* (if
    available), fresh
    or dried
The broth
The garnish (see above)
	Add the tortilla pieces and *epazote* to the broth and simmer for about 5 minutes; the tortillas should be soft but not falling apart.
	
	Garnish each bowl of soup with some of the cheese and a sprinkling of the chilies.

You may prefer to hand round the cheese and chilies separately, so that each person can garnish his own soup.

In Mexico *queso Chihuahua* would be used.

Tortilla Ball Soup

6 SERVINGS

The temptation, I think, might be to compare these with matzo balls, which can be deliciously light and delicate. These are much more solid, but have a nice grainy texture and a gentle corn flavor.

Have ready:

6 cups of tomato-chicken broth (see preceding recipe)
Finely chopped fresh coriander or parsley
⅓ cup Prepared Sour Cream (see page 27)

A blender
12 stale tortillas, dried
½ cup hot milk
½ cup finely grated
   Sardo cheese (about
   1½ ounces)
¼ teaspoon salt
1 egg, well beaten

Break the tortillas into small pieces and blend until they are reduced to a fine texture, but not to a powder; this amount will make about 1 cup. Add the rest of the ingredients and knead the dough well, then set it aside for several hours or overnight, to allow the tortilla particles to soften.

¼ cup cold milk,
   approximately

Again knead the dough well, adding the cold milk. Roll the dough evenly into one long piece; divide this into 12 pieces, and each piece into half again. Roll the pieces into small balls about 1 inch in diameter.

A frying pan
Melted lard or peanut
   or safflower oil to
   a depth of ¼ inch
Paper toweling
The heated broth
The chopped coriander
   or parsley
The sour cream

Heat the lard and fry the balls *very gently*, turning them from time to time until they are a golden brown—about 5 minutes. Drain well. Put the balls into the broth, bring to a boil, then reduce the heat and simmer for about 2 minutes.

Serve in individual bowls—4 balls per serving, 1 spoonful of the cream, and some chopped coriander.

Tortilla and Black Bean Soup

6 SERVINGS

Have ready:

½ pound cooked black beans (see page 18); this should measure 2 cups
    beans
 4 cups broth from cooking the beans (add water if necessary to make 4
    cups)
 9 stale tortillas, cut into thin strips:
 6 tablespoons finely grated Romano or Sardo cheese

A heavy saucepan
 6 ounces bacon (half
    fat, half lean)

Cut the bacon into very small pieces, then cook over a low flame until the fat renders out; do not let it brown.

The cooked beans
 2 cups of the bean
    broth
¼ medium onion,
    roughly chopped

Blend the beans with the broth and onion until smooth.

 4 whole *chiles serranos*
    or any fresh green
    chilies

Add the bean puree and whole chilies to the bacon in the pan and cook over a medium flame, scraping the bottom and sides of the pan almost constantly, for about 8 minutes.

The remaining bean
    broth
 2 sprigs *epazote*
    (optional)

Add the rest of the broth and the *epazote* and bring to a boil, then remove from the heat and keep warm.

A frying pan
Peanut or safflower oil
    to a depth of ½
    inch
The tortilla pieces
Paper toweling

Meanwhile, heat the oil and fry the tortilla pieces, about one third at a time, until they are stiff but not brown. Drain well and add to the soup.

The grated cheese

Simmer the soup for 5 minutes, then serve garnished with the cheese.

The base for the soup can be made ahead and even frozen.

    In Mexico *queso añejo* would be used.

    Epazote has a distinctive flavor, one that complements wonderfully the gentle flavor of the beans. Green coriander leaves would be an interesting, if untraditional, substitute for the *epazote*.

Casseroles

"Tortillas are soft cakes made of maize, or Indian corn;
they constitute the principal food of the poor and resemble our pikelets; they are wholesome, nutritious and
good, and when eaten warm, I considered them a deli-
cacy."

—Six Months Residence and Travel in Mexico
by W. H. Bullock (1824)

——◆——

Here is an assortment of Mexican *budines* (puddings), *sopas secas* ("dry soups"
or pastas), *taquitos al horno* (baked *tacos*), and *chilaquiles*, which have one
thing in common—they are all cooked in the same way. All are tortilla dishes—
tortillas filled and rolled, cut into strips, fried, and baked in layers with sauces,
cheese, and meat or vegetable fillings. They are all rather concentrated, some of
them rather rich. Some could be served just with a salad, a meal in themselves,
while others would make a good accompaniment to plainly cooked meats,
poultry, or fish. (Note that the following chapter deals with *chilaquiles* cooked
in a different way.)

Much will depend on the quality of the tortillas available to you (see page 33). And although the recipes have been test cooked with frozen and fresh tortillas, the behavior of every type across the country cannot be anticipated, and slight adjustments may have to be made in the amount of liquid in the sauces and cooking time in the oven. When the casserole is ready, it should be bubbling from the bottom, where the tortillas should be soft but not falling apart; on top they will still be slightly chewy. Once the casserole has been assembled it should be cooked and served or it tends to be soggy.

Tortilla Casserole

4 SERVINGS

A casserole of tortillas in tomato sauce known in Mexico as a "dry soup," which can be served as you would a pasta course, alone or with simply cooked meats, fish, or chicken.

Have ready:

12 stale tortillas cut into strips:
A greased ovenproof dish (ideally 5 × 9½ × 3)
 4 ounces Muenster, mild Cheddar, or similar cheese, grated (about 1 heaped cup)
 2 tablespoons finely chopped parsley (optional)
 1 cup Prepared Sour Cream (see page 27)
 ⅓ cup broth or hot water

A blender
 2 cups canned, drained tomatoes
 ¼ medium onion
 1 large clove garlic, peeled
 ¾ teaspoon salt, or to taste

Blend the tomatoes with the rest of the ingredients until smooth.

A frying pan
 2 tablespoons peanut or safflower oil

Heat the oil and fry the sauce over a fairly high flame to reduce and season—about 4 minutes. Remove from the heat and set in a warm place.

A frying pan
Peanut or safflower oil to a depth of ½ inch

Heat the oil and fry the tortilla pieces, about one-third at a time so they will cook evenly, until they are just stiffening but not brown. Drain well.

The tortilla pieces
Paper toweling

Preheat the oven to 375 degrees.

The prepared dish
The tomato sauce
The grated cheese
The broth

Put one third of the tortilla pieces at the bottom of the dish; sprinkle with ⅓ cup of the sauce and one third of the cheese. Repeat with half of the remaining tortillas, sauce, and cheese, then top off with the remaining ingredients. Moisten the top layer with the broth. Cover the dish with foil and set in the top level of the oven for about 15 to 20 minutes, or until heated through and bubbling. (The liquid should have been absorbed and the tortilla pieces *just* soft, not falling apart,at the bottom and still a little chewy on top. Slight adjustments may be needed to suit the tortillas that are available to you.)

The parsley
The sour cream

Serve: garnished with the parsley, if you like it. Hand round the sour cream separately.

Canned tomatoes actually give a better flavor to this casserole—unless, of course, you have access to sweet, fresh, vine-ripened tomatoes. More salt will be necessary if fresh tomatoes are used, in which case use about 1¼ pounds.

In Mexico *queso Chihuahua* or *queso fresco* is used.

Tortilla and Vegetable Casserole

4 SERVINGS

The original recipe called for *chorizo*, but I find it much more delicious without, since the flavor of the vegetables is not overpowered. It can be served as a separate course, alone or with plainly broiled meats, fish, or roast chicken.

Have ready:

12　tortillas, cut into strips, thus:
An ovenproof serving dish (8 × 8 × 2)
　1　cup cooked peas (6 ounces); if frozen peas are used, simply defrost them
　1　cup cooked, diced carrot (about 8 ounces)

1 cup cooked green beans (about 6 ounces), cut into small pieces
4 ounces mild Cheddar, Muenster, or similar cheese, grated (about 1 heaped
  cup)

A frying pan
1½ tablespoons peanut
  or safflower oil
1 medium onion,
  thinly sliced
	Heat the oil and cook the onion gently until soft; do not brown.

A blender
2 medium tomatoes,
  broiled (see page
  29) or 1¼ cups
  canned, drained
½ teaspoon salt
⅔ cup vegetable water
  or chicken broth
	Blend the tomatoes briefly, then add, with the salt, to the onions in the pan. Cook over a fairly high flame, stirring from time to time, until it reduces—about 3 minutes. Add the vegetable water or broth and cook for a minute or so longer, then set aside.

Peanut or safflower oil to **a depth of ½ inch** **The tortilla pieces** **Paper toweling**	Heat the oil and fry the tortilla pieces, about one third at a time so they fry evenly, until just beginning to stiffen, not brown. Drain well.
	Preheat the oven to 375 degrees.
The prepared dish **The vegetables, well-** **seasoned** **The tomato sauce**	Spread half of the tortilla pieces over the bottom of the dish. Sprinkle with about one third of the sauce, cover with the vegetables, the rest of the tortillas, and finally the rest of the sauce. Cover the dish with foil and bake for about 20 minutes, or until the bottom tortillas are soft but not falling apart and the top ones are still slightly chewy. Remove the foil.
The grated cheese	Sprinkle the cheese over the top of the casserole and return the dish to the oven just until the cheese melts.

Once this casserole is assembled it should be cooked and served, or it will become a little soggy.

Be sure not to overcook the vegetables—they should be just tender, almost crisp, so that they do not become mushy during baking.

Mushroom Pudding

4 SERVINGS

The original recipe calls for *huitlacoche,* or the delicious fungus that grows on corn (see *The Cuisines of Mexico* page 23), which is pure ambrosia by any worldly standards but hard to come by outside of Mexico, where it is highly esteemed. Mushrooms have been cheap and plentiful, and this recipe provides a delicious variation to the usual ways of preparing them.

You may use more or less chilies, depending on your taste.

Have ready:

12 stale tortillas cut into fours
A lightly greased ovenproof dish (9¼ × 5½ × 3)
 4 ounces mild Cheddar, Muenster, or jack cheese, grated (about 1 heaped cup)

1 pound mushrooms

Rinse the mushrooms several times under running water to wash away any gritty soil that has stuck to the base of the stems. Slice thin.

A frying pan
 2 tablespoons peanut or safflower oil
⅔ medium onion, thinly sliced
 2 cloves garlic, peeled and finely chopped
 3 *chiles serranos* or any fresh, green chilies, finely chopped
½ teaspoon salt, or to taste
 1 large sprig *epazote* or parsley, leaves only, roughly chopped

Heat the oil and fry the onion and garlic for 2 minutes, stirring constantly—they should not brown. Add the mushrooms, chilies and salt, then cover the pan and cook over medium heat until the mushrooms are tender—about 20 minutes; they should be juicy. Add the *epazote* and cook for 1 minute more. Set aside.

A blender
 1 pound tomatoes, skinned and chopped, or 2 cups canned, drained
⅓ medium onion, roughly chopped

Blend the ingredients together until smooth.

1 clove garlic, peeled
¾ teaspoon salt, or to
    taste

A frying pan
 1 tablespoon peanut or
    safflower oil

Heat the oil and cook the sauce over a fairly high flame, stirring it almost constantly, for about 4 minutes. It should reduce and season.

A frying pan
Peanut or safflower oil to
    a depth of ½ inch
The tortilla pieces
Paper toweling

Heat the oil and fry the tortillas, about one third at a time so they fry evenly, until they are just becoming stiff but do not harden and brown. Drain on paper toweling.

Preheat the oven to 375 degrees.

The prepared dish
The mushroom mixture
The grated cheese
The sauce

Put one third of the tortilla pieces at the bottom of the dish, half of the mushroom mixture, one third of the cheese, and ⅓ cup sauce. Repeat the layers and top off with the rest of the cheese, sauce, and any mushroom juice left in the pan. Bake until well heated through and bubbling—about 20 to 25 minutes.

Baked Shrimp Tacos (*from Tampico*)

4 SERVINGS

Have ready:

An ovenproof serving dish (ideally 10 × 6 × 3); the tacos should fit snugly in
   2 layers)
12 tortillas
 4 ounces mild Cheddar, Muenster, or similar cheese, grated (about 1 heaped
   cup)
⅔ cup Prepared Sour Cream (see page 27)
 2 tablespoons roughly chopped parsley or coriander leaves
 1 medium onion, thinly sliced

A blender
1¼ pounds tomatoes,
  skinned, seeded, and
  chopped, or 2 cups
  canned, drained
	Blend the tomatoes until smooth. Set aside.

A frying pan
 3 tablespoons peanut
   or safflower oil
½ medium onion,
   finely chopped
½ pound shrimp,
   peeled and deveined
 3 small red bliss or
   other waxy potatoes
   (½ pound), cooked
   and diced
 2 *chiles jalapeños* or
   any fresh, green
   chilies, cut into thin
   strips (optional)
¾ teaspoon salt
	Heat the oil and fry the onion gently, without browning, until soft. Cut each of the shrimp into 4 pieces and add to the pan, along with the potatoes, chili strips, and salt. Fry over a fairly high flame for about 2 minutes, stirring all the time.

¾ cup of the tomato puree	Add the puree and continue cooking over a medium flame, stirring from time to time, until the sauce is reduced—about 4 minutes. Set aside and keep warm.
A frying pan 2 tablespoons peanut or safflower oil	Heat the oil. Meanwhile, blend the remaining tomato puree with the onion and fry it over a fairly high flame, stirring from time to time,

A blender
The remaining tomato
    puree
⅓ medium onion
½ teaspoon salt, or to
    taste

until it has reduced a little—about 4 minutes. Set aside and keep warm.

A frying pan
Peanut or safflower oil to
    a depth of ¼ inch
The tortillas
Paper toweling

Heat the oil and fry the tortillas, one by one, lightly on both sides (see note for *enchiladas,* page 112). Drain well and keep warm until you have done them all.

The shrimp-potato filling
The prepared dish
The grated cheese
The tomato sauce

Put a large spoonful of the shrimp-potato mixture onto each tortilla. Roll up loosely and place six of them in one layer on the bottom of the dish. Sprinkle with half the cheese and cover with one third of the tomato sauce. Cover with another layer of the *tacos,* the rest of the sauce, and then the cheese. Cover the dish with foil and bake for about 10 minutes, until well heated through and bubbling. Take care not to overcook—the tortillas should be soft but not disintegrating.

The sour cream
The chopped parsley
The chopped onion

Garnish and serve immediately.

The original recipe did not call for the onion and parsley (or coriander) but I like their crisp freshness, which is a good foil for the soft texture of the dish.

Once assembled the dish should be baked and served; otherwise it will become mushy.

Baked Tacos Lagunera (*from Coahuila*)

4 SERVINGS

Have ready:

12 tortillas (see Enchiladas, Method I, page 115)

An ovenproof serving dish (ideally 10 × 6 × 3; the tacos should fit snugly in 2 layers)

¾ cup grated mild Cheddar, Muenster, or similar cheese (about 3 ounces)

¾ cup Prepared Sour Cream (see page 27)

½ medium onion, finely chopped (optional)

2 tablespoons chopped parsley (optional)

A frying pan
  2 tablespoons peanut or safflower oil
  1 medium onion, thinly sliced
  4 *chiles poblanos*, peeled and cleaned (see page 30), or 6 canned, peeled green chilies (2 four-ounce cans), seeded
	Heat the oil and fry the onion gently, without browning, until soft. Cut the chilies into strips, add them to the pan, and cook for about 3 minutes, stirring almost constantly. Remove from the pan and set aside.

A blender 2 medium tomatoes (¾ pound), broiled (see page 29), or 1½ cups canned, drained	Blend the tomatoes briefly.
A frying pan 1½ tablespoons peanut or safflower oil ½ teaspoon salt, or to taste Freshly ground black pepper	Heat the oil in the pan. Add the tomatoes and fry over a fairly high flame, stirring from time to time until reduced—about 5 minutes. Season, then add to the onion-chili mixture and keep warm.
Peanut or safflower oil to a depth of ¼ inch The tortillas Paper toweling	Heat the oil and fry the tortillas lightly on both sides. Drain well. Preheat the oven to 350 degrees.

The filling
The prepared dish
The grated cheese
The sour cream
The chopped onion
The chopped parsley

Put a large spoonful of the filling onto each tortilla. Roll up loosely and place a layer of six on the bottom of the dish. Sprinkle half of the cheese over them; cover with the rest of the *tacos* and cheese. Cover the dish tightly with foil and bake for about 10 minutes (the tortillas should be soft but not disintegrating). Pour the sour cream over and garnish with the onion and parsley, if desired.

Once assembled, the dish must be baked and served. If it has to stand it will become very mushy.

The original recipe calls for cream and *queso fresco* between the layers (see my note about sour cream on page 27) and is not garnished with onions and parsley, though it is within the Mexican tradition—and personally, I like something fresh and crisp on top.

"Student Chilaquiles" (*from Oaxaca*)

In the region of Mexico where the states of Puebla, Guerrero, and Oaxaca converge, many of the dishes are quite sweet; pineapple, sugar, raisins, and candied fruits are often used in the sauces and meat fillings. I find the chili sauce in the recipe below fragrant and quite addictive.

This is a very substantial dish and should be served with just a plain green salad.

Have ready:

12 stale tortillas, each cut into 6 pieces like a pie: ⊗
 1 heaped cup (about ¾ pound) cooked and shredded chicken or pork (see page 56)
An ovenproof serving dish (5 × 9½ × 3)
½ cup crumbled farmer cheese (about 3 ounces)

THE SAUCE

A small bowl
 4 *chiles anchos*, toasted and cleaned (see page 30)
Hot water to cover
A blender
⅓ medium onion
 2 cloves garlic, peeled
¼-inch piece of cinnamon bark
 1 clove
 3 peppercorns
 2 teaspoons granulated sugar
 1 teaspoon salt
½ cup water

Cover the chilies with hot water and leave them to soak for about 20 minutes. Drain and transfer to the blender jar, then add the rest of the ingredients and blend until smooth. It will be a thick puree.

A frying pan
 2 tablespoons peanut or safflower oil
¾ cup chicken or pork broth, approximately (see note below)

Heat the oil and cook the sauce over a medium flame, scraping and stirring constantly for about 5 minutes; it will be very thick. Add the broth and heat through—the sauce should lightly coat the back of a wooden spoon. Set aside.

THE FILLING

A blender
 1 medium tomato (6
   ounces), broiled
   (see page 29) or ¾
   cup canned, drained
 1 clove garlic, peeled
 ¼ medium onion

Blend the tomatoes with the rest of the ingredients until smooth.

A frying pan
 1 tablespoon peanut oil

Heat the oil and cook the tomato puree over a fairly high flame for about 3 minutes, stirring well all the time.

The cooked meat
 2 tablespoons raisins
 8 pitted green olives,
   roughly chopped
 ½ teaspoon salt

Add the rest of the ingredients and cook over a medium flame, stirring from time to time, for about 5 minutes. The mixture should be well seasoned and almost dry. Set aside.

THE ASSEMBLY

A frying pan
**Peanut or safflower oil to
   a depth of ½ inch**
The tortilla pieces
Paper toweling

Preheat the oven to 350 degrees.

Heat the oil and fry the tortilla pieces, about one third at a time so they are evenly cooked, until they begin to stiffen but do not brown. Drain well.

The serving dish
The sauce
The filling

Spread one third of the tortillas over the bottom of the dish, then one half of the filling and one third of the sauce. Repeat the layers and top off with the rest of the tortillas and sauce. Cover the dish tightly with foil and bake for about 20 minutes. (As with all *chilaquile* dishes, the tortillas should be slightly chewy.)

The farmer cheese

Sprinkle with the cheese and serve immediately.

Once assembled, the dish should be baked and served or it will become very mushy.

It is very difficult to give the exact amount of broth needed to dilute the sauce, since there is such a difference in the size and fleshiness of the chilies.

If you are using frozen tortillas that are very thin, then add about 3 more. The sauce and filling together are delicious but strong and concentrated, and this really come off best when the tortillas are rather thick and mealy.

In Mexico *queso fresco* would be used.

Torta Moctezuma

4 SERVINGS

There are so many versions of this type of casserole—Moctezuma pie, *budín Azteca, torta Huasteca,* and the various *tamal* pies invented, I would imagine, to use up leftovers. They are all rather solid and luscious, and certainly not recommended for calorie counters.

Have ready:

  1 pound pork cooked and shredded (about 1⅓ cups) (see page 56), broth reserved
 12 stale tortillas, each cut into 4 pieces
An ovenproof serving dish (should be about 3 inches deep; I use a round casserole about 9 inches in diameter, which is perfect. This recipe somehow won't fit into any of the more conventional sizes.)
  1 heaped cup grated mild Cheddar, Muenster, or similar cheese (about 4 ounces)
1½ cups shredded lettuce, lightly dressed with oil and vinegar
  6 large radishes, thinly sliced

A frying pan
 2 tablespoons peanut or safflower oil
⅓ medium onion, finely chopped
 2 cloves garlic, peeled and finely chopped
The shredded meat

Heat the oil. Add the garlic, onion, and meat and fry, stirring almost constantly, until the meat begins to brown—about 4 minutes.

A blender
 1 pound tomatoes, broiled (see page 29), or 2 cups canned, drained
 5 *chiles poblanos,* or

Blend the tomatoes briefly, then add them to the pan, along with the chili strips and salt. Let the mixture cook over a medium flame, stirring it from time to time, until some of the sauce is reduced—8 minutes for broiled fresh tomatoes, 10 to 12 minutes for canned

1 seven-ounce can peeled green chilies, seeded and cut into strips
1 teaspoon salt
⅓ cup broth from the meat

tomatoes. Then add the broth, adjust the seasoning, and cook for a minute or two more. Set aside.

A frying pan
Peanut or safflower oil to a depth of ½ inch
A bowl
An egg beater
4 eggs
½ teaspoon salt
The tortilla pieces
½ cup all-purpose flour, approximately
Paper toweling

Heat the oil. Beat the eggs together with the salt until frothy. Dust the tortilla pieces lightly with the flour, then dip into the beaten egg—very little should adhere to the tortilla—and fry quickly (see note below) until golden—about 1 minute on either side if your oil is the correct temperature. Drain well.

Preheat the oven to 350 degrees.

The serving dish
The meat mixture
The grated cheese

Spread one third of the tortilla pieces over the bottom of the dish, followed by half of the meat mixture and one third of the cheese; repeat the layers and top off with the remaining tortillas and cheese. Cover the dish tightly with foil and bake for about 20 minutes, until the casserole is bubbling; the tortillas at the bottom should be soft and on top still a little bit chewy.

The shredded lettuce
The radish slices

Garnish each serving with lettuce and radish slices.

Once assembled, the dish should be cooked and served. It becomes soggy if it stands any length of time.

When frying the tortilla pieces, use both a large spatula and a pair of tongs. When the pieces are golden, gather them up, several at a time, and let them drain a little over the pan. Work quickly so you won't get bored. Halfway through you will think that the eggs are running out—make them do; don't forget that you are *not* cooking *chiles rellenos*—nobody's going to see that the tortillas are not perfectly covered.

Sweet Red Pepper Casserole

4 SERVINGS

This is a sort of variation on a theme of tortilla casseroles most probably evolved in Mexico City. It could be served alone as a pasta, or with eggs for brunch, or as an accompaniment to plainly broiled fish or meat.

Have ready:

12 stale tortillas, cut into strips, thus:
An ovenproof serving dish ($9\frac{1}{2} \times 5\frac{1}{2} \times 3$)
 1 cup Prepared Sour Cream (see page 27)

A frying pan
1½ tablespoons peanut
      or safflower oil
 ½ medium onion,
      thinly sliced

Heat the oil and cook the onion gently until soft; do not brown.

A blender
  2 medium tomatoes
       (¾ pound) broiled,
       or 1½ cups canned,
       drained
  1 clove garlic, peeled
 ½ teaspoon salt

Blend the tomatoes with the garlic, then add to the onions with the salt and cook over a fairly high flame, stirring and scraping the bottom of the pan from time to time until it has reduced—about 3 minutes. Set aside.

A frying pan
Peanut or safflower oil to
      a depth of ½ inch
The tortilla pieces
Paper toweling

Heat the oil and fry the tortilla strips, about one third at a time so that they fry evenly, until just stiffening but not hard. Drain well.

The prepared dish
The sauce
 ¾ cup crumbled farmer
      cheese (about 4
      ounces)
  2 four-ounce cans
      peeled pimientos,
      cut into strips
      (about 1 cup)

Spread one-third of the tortilla pieces over the bottom of the dish, then add half the pepper strips, half the cheese, and one third of the sauce. Repeat the layers and finish off with the rest of the tortillas and sauce.

Preheat the oven to 375 degrees.

The sour cream

Cover the dish with foil and bake for about 15 to 20 minutes (the tortillas underneath should be soft but not falling apart while those on top will still be a little chewy). Serve each portion with a little of the sour cream.

Take care when choosing canned pimientos or tomatoes. A sharp canning liquid can make the dish too acidy.

If you wish to use fresh red peppers, you will need about 4 large ones; prepare them as you would chili strips (see page 30).

If you can be bothered to make your own sour cream, add some between the layers; commercial sour cream, however, will curdle in the oven.

In Mexico *queso fresco* would be used.

Chilaquiles

"Tortillas, which are the common food of the people, and which are merely maize cakes mixed with a little lime, and of the form and size of what we call scones. I find them rather good when hot and fresh-baked but insipid by themselves. They have been in use all through this country since the earliest ages of its history, without any change in the manner of baking them, excepting that for the noble Mexicans in former days, they used to be kneaded with various medicinal plants, supposed to render them more wholesome. They are considered particularly palatable with chile, to endure which, in the quantities it is eaten here, it seems to me necessary to have a throat lined with tin."

—Life in Mexico
by Frances Calderón de la Barca (1838)

————◦•◦————

Even in the homogenized-looking breakfast rooms of the most modern Mexico City hotels, where the menu is "internacional," your breakfast eggs will in all probability be served with a little dollop of rather dried-up-looking tortillas cooked in a *picante* sauce—*chilaquiles* in their simplest form, and despite their appearance, very good.

The much-respected *Diccionario de Aztequisimos* gives a complicated derivation from *nahuatl* words and then finishes up with "*chilaquil:* broken-up old sombrero." As complicated and delightful as the name sounds, it is simply a way of using up old tortillas. There are as many recipes for them as there are cooks who find themselves with supper to provide out of old tortillas, leftover sauces, and meats.

Traditionally, the tortillas are torn into pieces, fried briefly, and cooked for a short time in a chili sauce. They are garnished lavishly very often, and sometimes one begins to wonder whether that isn't more important than the *chilaquiles* themselves. But in actual fact the garnishes provide crisp, sharp countertastes and textures.

GENERAL NOTES

1. Tortillas for *chilaquiles* should be stale, but they should be cut before they become too stiff. Pile several, one on top of the other, and cut them through with a heavy knife, or a Chinese cleaver, into 6 pieces like a pie. If the tortillas are too fresh, spread them onto a baking sheet and dry them out in a slow oven for 20 minutes to 1 hour, depending on thickness.

2. Fry a small quantity of the tortilla pieces at a time, so that they cover the bottom of the pan in one layer, to ensure even cooking. They should be fried until they are just beginning to stiffen; be careful not to let them become crisp and brown or they will not reach the correct chewy consistency in the next cooking stage (i.e., in the sauce).

3. Once you have added the tortillas to the sauce, keep stirring and scraping the bottom of the pan as the mixture will stick and burn easily. If by the time the sauce has been absorbed the tortillas are still rather hard, lower the flame, cover the pan, and cook for a few minutes longer. Or you may need to add a little bit of water or broth to the sauce.

4. There is no hard and fast rule about ingredients. Use up whatever you have handy.

Green Chilaquiles (*from Tampico*)

4 TO 6 SERVINGS

Have ready:

12 stale tortillas, cut into 6 pieces, thus: ⊗
A warmed serving dish (8 × 8 × 2) or serving platter
¾ cup crumbled, well-salted farmer cheese
½ medium onion, finely chopped
 2 hard-boiled eggs, sliced
 6 large radishes, thinly sliced
 2 tablespoons roughly chopped coriander leaves

A blender
½ pound Mexican green tomatoes, cooked (see page 25), or 1 cup canned, drained and then blended with ⅓ cup water and a pinch of sugar
3 *chiles poblanos*, peeled and cleaned (see page 30), or 5 canned, peeled green chilies, seeded
2 sprigs *epazote*, leaves only
3 sprigs coriander, leaves only
⅓ medium onion, roughly chopped
¾ teaspoon salt

Blend the green tomatoes with the rest of the ingredients until smooth.

1 tablespoon peanut or safflower oil
1 cup chicken broth

Heat the oil and fry the sauce over a medium flame, stirring constantly, for 5 minutes. Add the broth and continue cooking for 1 minute more, then remove from the heat and set aside.

A frying pan
Peanut or safflower oil to a depth of ½ inch
The tortilla pieces
Paper toweling

Heat the oil and fry the tortillas pieces, about one third at a time so they will be evenly cooked, until they just begin to stiffen but do not brown. Drain well.

The sauce

The garnish (see above)

Return the sauce to the heat and bring to a boil; stir in the tortilla pieces and cook them over a medium flame, scraping the bottom of the pan almost constantly, until most of the liquid has been absorbed and the tortillas *just* softening—5 to 8 minutes. Garnish with the cheese, onion, egg, radishes, and coriander and serve immediately.

In Mexico *queso fresco* would be used.

Tortilla and Chorizo "Dry Soup"

4 SERVINGS

This method of cooking is exactly the same as that for *chilaquiles*, but there are no chilies in the sauce, so technically it is, according to the Mexicans, a "dry soup."

Have ready:

12 stale tortillas, cut into strips, thus: ⊞
A warmed serving dish or platter
½ cup crumbled farmer cheese (about 3 ounces)
½ medium onion, thinly sliced

A frying pan
  2 *chorizos*, skinned
    and crumbled
  1 tablespoon melted
    lard or peanut or
    safflower oil

Cook the *chorizos* gently in the lard for about 4 minutes, stirring from time to time, then remove the sausage meat and reserve the fat.

A blender
  2 medium tomatoes
    (about 10 ounces),
    skinned and
    chopped, or 1¼
    cups canned,
    drained
¼ medium onion,
    roughly chopped
The frying pan
The reserved *chorizo* fat

Blend the tomatoes with the onion, then cook the puree in 1 tablespoon of the *chorizo* fat over a fairly high flame for about 3 minutes, stirring almost constantly. Remove from the heat and set aside.

(continued)

A frying pan
Peanut or safflower oil to
      a depth of ½ inch
The tortilla pieces
Paper toweling

Heat the oil and fry the tortilla pieces, about one-third at a time so they are cooked evenly, until they just begin to stiffen but do not brown. Drain well.

The tomato sauce
The *chorizo* pieces
 1 cup broth
 2 sprigs fresh mint, or
      6 to 8 dried leaves
½ teaspoon salt, or to
      taste

Combine the tortilla pieces with the sauce, add all the other ingredients, and cook gently, stirring the mixture from time to time and scraping the bottom of the pan until the sauce has thickened a little and the tortillas are soft but not falling apart—from 5 to 8 minutes.

The farmer cheese
The sliced onion

Garnish with the cheese and onion slices and serve immediately.

Chilaquiles from Aguascalientes

4 SERVINGS

The *chiles chipotles* lend a pungent and smoky flavor to the sauce here. Like many other *chilaquile* dishes, this would be good served with eggs for brunch, or leaving out the *chorizo*, with plain roasted chicken and a green salad.

Have ready:

12 stale tortillas cut into 6 pieces, thus: ⊗
 3 *chorizos*, skinned, crumbled, and fried (see page 22)
½ pound farmer cheese, crumbled (about 1½ cups)
An ovenproof dish (about 8 × 5 × 3)
⅔ medium onion, thinly sliced
 1 tablespoon roughly chopped coriander leaves (optional)

A blender
½ four-ounce can
      chiles chipotles
 2 sprigs coriander,
      leaves only
⅓ medium onion
1½ tablespoons sesame
      seeds, toasted (see
      page 27)

Blend all the ingredients until smooth.

⅛ teaspoon dried
    oregano
⅔ cup cooked fresh or
    canned, drained
    Mexican green
    tomatoes (see page
    25), ⅓ cup water
    (if canned green
    tomatoes are used),
    and a pinch of sugar
2 cloves garlic, peeled
1 teaspoon salt
1 medium tomato,
    broiled (see page
    29), or ⅔ cup
    canned, drained

A frying pan
  **2 tablespoons peanut
    or safflower oil**

Heat the oil and cook the sauce over a fairly high flame, stirring and scraping the bottom for about 5 minutes. Remove from the heat and set aside. Preheat the oven to 350 degrees.

A frying pan
**Peanut or safflower oil to
  a depth of ½ inch**
The tortilla pieces
Paper toweling

Heat the oil and fry the tortilla pieces, about one-third at a time so they are evenly cooked, until they just begin to stiffen but do not brown. Drain well.

The ovenproof dish
The *chorizos*
The farmer cheese
The sauce

The sliced onion
The chopped coriander

Put one-third of the tortillas at the bottom of the dish, half the *chorizos* and cheese and ⅓ cup of the sauce. Repeat the layers and top off with the rest of the tortillas and sauce. Cover the dish with foil and bake for about 15 to 20 minutes, or until well heated through and the tortillas are *just* soft. Garnish with the onion and coriander and serve.

If the *chorizo* flavor is too strong, then use only 1 chorizo and a cupful of cooked and shredded pork.

In Mexico *queso fresco* would be used.

Chilaquiles from Veracruz

4 SERVINGS

This is one of the most delicious versions of *chilaquiles*. Everything can, of course, be prepared ahead of time and the sauce reheated and cooked with tortilla pieces at the last moment. With a plain green salad it makes a most satisfying meal.

Have ready:

12 stale tortillas, cut into 6 pieces, thus: ⊗
A warmed serving dish (about 8 × 8 × 2)
  1 cup Prepared Sour Cream (see page 27)
  1 small avocado, peeled, cut into small squares, and dressed with a vinai-grette
  1 cup Pickled Onion Rings (see page 43)
  ½ cup crumbled farmer cheese (about 3 ounces)

A saucepan
  1 whole chicken breast, or 2 large legs, if preferred
  1 teaspoon salt
  1 large clove garlic, peeled
  ⅓ onion, roughly sliced
  2 sprigs fresh coriander
  2 sprigs fresh mint, or 1 scant tablespoon dried
  2 cups cold water

Put all the ingredients into the saucepan. Bring to a boil, then lower the flame and simmer until the chicken is just tender—about 20 minutes for breast, 25 or more for legs. Allow the chicken to cool off in the broth. When the meat is cool enough to handle, take it from the bones and shred it. Strain and reserve the broth.

A frying pan
  2 tablespoons peanut or safflower oil
  1 *chile ancho*
A small bowl
Hot water to cover

Heat the oil. Remove the seeds from the chili and fry it for about 1 minute on each side, flattening it down in the pan with a spatula. Remove the chili, cover it with hot water, and leave to soak for about 20 minutes. Leave the oil in the pan.

A blender
  1 large tomato (½ pound), skinned and chopped, or 1 cup canned, and drained

Transfer the chili to the blender jar, add the rest of the ingredients, and blend until smooth.

1 large clove garlic,
    peeled
½ teaspoon salt
¼ cup water

The frying pan	Reheat the oil and fry the sauce over a fairly high flame for about 3 minutes, scraping the bottom of the pan almost constantly. Add the broth and cook for 1 minute more. Adjust the seasoning, remove from the heat, and set aside.
The oil	
1 cup chicken broth	
Salt as necessary	
A frying pan	Heat the oil and fry the tortilla pieces, about one-third at a time so they cook evenly, until they just begin to stiffen but do not brown. Drain well.
Peanut or safflower oil to a depth of ½ inch	
The tortilla pieces	
Paper toweling	
The sauce	Return the sauce to the heat. As it begins to boil, stir in the tortillas and cook over a medium flame for about 5 to 8 minutes, or until most of the sauce has been absorbed and the tortilla pieces are just beginning to soften. Stir constantly or the sauce and tortillas will stick and burn.
The serving dish	Put the *chilaquiles* into the dish first, then add the cream, the chicken, the avocado, the onion rings, and lastly the cheese. Serve immediately.
The sour cream	
The cooked chicken	
The avocado squares	
The pickled onion rings	
The farmer cheese	

This is not a *picante* dish, but you may leave the seeds and veins in the chili to give it a little more kick.

In Mexico *queso fresco* would be used.

Chilaquiles from Guanajuato

4 SERVINGS

This is a strong, *picante* dish with a great flavor.

Have ready:

12 stale tortillas, cut into 6 wedge-shaped pieces: ⊗
A warmed serving platter or ovenproof dish (about 8 × 8 × 2)
 6 ounces mild Cheddar, Muenster, or jack cheese thinly sliced
⅔ medium onion, finely chopped

A blender
 6 *chiles guajillos*,
     toasted and cleaned
     (see page 30)
¾ pound Mexican
     green tomatoes,
     cooked (see page
     25), or 1½ cups
     canned, drained and
     then blended with
     ½ cup water and a
     pinch of sugar
¾ teaspoon salt
⅓ medium onion
 2 cloves garlic, peeled

Put the chiles into the blender jar. Add the rest of the ingredients and blend until quite smooth.

A frying pan
 2 tablespoons peanut
     or safflower oil

Heat the oil and fry the sauce over a medium flame for about 5 minutes, scraping the bottom of the pan almost constantly. Remove from the heat and set aside.

A frying pan
Peanut or safflower oil to
     a depth of ½ inch
The tortilla pieces
Paper toweling

Heat the oil and fry the tortillas, about one third at a time so they are cooked evenly, until they just begin to stiffen but do not brown. Drain well.

Preheat the broiler or oven.

The sauce	Return the sauce to the heat and bring to the boiling point. Stir in the tortilla pieces and cook over a medium flame, stirring constantly, for about 8 minutes, or until they are just beginning to soften and some of the sauce has been absorbed. (Take care, as the sauce sticks and burns easily.) Transfer the *chilaquiles* to the serving dish. Cover with the cheese, then run the dish under a hot broiler or into the oven until the cheese just begins to melt. Garnish with the onion and serve.
The serving dish	
The cheese	
The chopped onion	

Try serving this dish with fried eggs on top for brunch; it is an almost surefire way to kill a hangover. It is also very good served with sour cream on top, with scrambled eggs, with plain roasted chicken.

A note of warning about *chiles guajillos*: they are extremely hot. If you have sensitive skin wear plastic gloves when removing the seeds and veins. And if you haven't worn gloves and your fingers are stinging, wash them several times in hot, soapy water, scrubbing well under the nails.

Masa Fantasies

I rather like this condescending description of a tortilla—it is a translation from *Nuevo Cocinero Mejicano*, published by Bouret in Paris in 1878. I have tried to retain the tone of the language.

Tortilla is the name given to the bread made of corn that nourished the ancient inhabitants of this continent and is used to this day by their descendants, be they poor or well-to-do. It is served by preference in some of the most prosperous homes in the countryside and the provinces. The way to make them is such common knowledge and so simple that it would be superfluous to describe it if this book were to be circulated only amongst ourselves. Like *atole* and other simple food, the preparation is so commonplace that there is not a single household here where it is not known. But since it is probable that this book will be read in other countries where corn is cultivated assiduously and is the principal food of the poor, it would be a service to humanity to describe here the simple and easy way to make this cheap, wholesome and delicious bread.

Gordas, sopes, chalupas, quesadillas—enchanting names, but these are just a few of the *masa* fantasies, for wherever you travel in Mexico there are the specialties of that region—the *garnachas* of Yucatán and Veracruz, the *panuchos* of Yucatán and Campeche; the *bocadillos* of Oaxaca; *bocoles* of Tamaulipas; and the *tlacoyos, memelas, picadas,* and *pelliscadas* of central Mexico. They are all variations on a theme—corn dough flattened into little cakes, thick or thin, fried or toasted, some reddened with dried chilies, enriched with creamy cheese or marrow fat, stuffed with beans, or seasoned with dried shrimps. Some are topped with shredded meats, crumbled cheese, doused with a fiery sauce and decorated colorfully with radish, tomato, or lettuce—or whatever is at hand. The corn dough is patted and coaxed into a hundred different little forms, enticing you to nibble from morning until night. These are just a few of the hundreds of variations on what the Mexicans call *antojitos*, "little whims."

Bean and Masa Snacks

4 TO 6 SERVINGS

A mixing bowl
1½ cups *masa harina* (see note below)
½ teaspoon salt
½ tablespoon lard
¾ cup water, more if necessary
¼ cup Refried Beans (black) (see page 18)

Mix the *masa harina* with the salt; add the lard and water and knead lightly to a soft dough. (You may need a little more water.) Divide the dough into 12 equal parts and roll into balls—they should be just under 1½ inches. Make a deep well with your thumb in the center of each ball and fill with 1 teaspoon of the bean paste.

A tortilla press (optional)
2 small polyethylene bags (optional)

Either using your palms or pressing lightly inside a tortilla press, flatten the balls to make a rather thick tortilla no more than 3½ inches in diameter. The beans should not be covered—there will be a black center to the dough.

A frying pan
Melted lard or peanut or safflower oil to a depth of ¼ inch
Paper toweling

Heat the lard and fry the dough for about 1½ minutes on either side, or until nicely browned. Drain and serve immediately with a *picante* sauce (see note below).

Prepared *masa* can be used with good results. Use ¾ pound and eliminate the *masa harina* and water.

These could hold for a few minutes in a 375-degree oven, but they do get a little dried out if left too long, and in a lower oven they will become soggy. Serve with any of the sauces on pages 39-41. Personally, I like the contrast of the Fresh Table Sauce (see page 40) with this recipe. If you use the Cooked Tomato Sauce (see page 39), then add the *chiles serranos* as suggested in the recipe.

GENERAL NOTES ON RED AND GREEN CHILI GORDAS

1. If you have any dried-up old tortillas, the following two recipes provide a unique and delicious way of using them up. Mexican recipe books will tell you to soak them in milk overnight and then grind them to a soft dough with a grinding stone and muller (*metate* and *mano*). Modern blenders cannot cope with this consistency—the blades will stick fast—and it may be too much trouble to assemble the meat grinder to do the job (and it certainly is a nuisance to clean). The best way, then, is to dry the tortillas literally to a crisp. Since one often doesn't think far enough ahead to let them dry out to that degree—and even if you did, it would be rather inconvenient to have them sitting around on trays in the kitchen for days—spread them out on baking sheets and dry them slowly in the oven, but without allowing them to brown. It may take from 45 minutes to 2 hours, depending on their thickness, how stale they are, and so forth. Then blend them—dry, of course—to a rough-textured flour. Once you have mixed the dough, it is preferable—although not absolutely necessary—to set it aside for at least 2 hours, so that the hard tortilla particles can soften a little.

2. If you refrigerate the dough overnight, bring it up to room temperature before making the *gordas*.

3. If the dough is kept for more than about 3 to 4 days it is likely to turn sour, so leftovers should be stored for any longer period in the freezing compartment of the refrigerator.

4. When you are frying the *gordas*, make sure that the fat is hot enough so it will not be absorbed by the dough, but not so hot as to seal the outside with a hard crust while the inside remains cold and uncooked.

5. They will hold in a 350-degree oven for about 20 minutes.

Red Chili Gordas

4 TO 6 SERVINGS

Have ready:

12 dried tortillas (see page 100)
1½ cups Cooked Tomato Sauce (see page 39)
1 medium onion, finely chopped
6 tablespoons finely grated Romano or Sardo cheese
1 cup Prepared Sour Cream (see page 27)
1½ cups shredded and dressed lettuce (see page 24)

A mixing bowl
1 *chile ancho*, toasted and cleaned (see page 30)
1½ cups hot milk

Cover the chili with the hot milk and soak for about 20 minutes. Blend until smooth, then transfer to a bowl.

A blender
A bowl
The tortillas
The ground chili
1 teaspoon salt

Break the tortillas into a perfectly dry blender jar and blend until finely ground—but not to a powder. Mix with the ground chili, then add the salt and knead the dough well. Set aside to soften for an hour or more if you have the time.

Roll the dough into 12 balls about 1½ inches in diameter. Flatten them to make cakes about 2 inches across and ¼ inch thick.

Preheat the oven to 350 degrees.

A frying pan
Melted lard or peanut or safflower oil to a depth of ¼ inch
Paper toweling

Heat the oil over a high flame, then lower the flame and gently fry the cakes, a few at a time, for about 3 minutes on each side. Drain well, then keep them warm in the oven while you fry the rest.

The garnish (see above)

Garnish each with a little of the tomato sauce, onion, cheese, and sour cream, then surround with the shredded lettuce and serve.

In Mexico *queso ranchero* would be used.

Green Chili Gordas (*from Zacatecas*)

4 TO 6 SERVINGS

Have ready:

12 dried tortillas (see page|100)
1½ cups Prepared Sour Cream (see page 27), Cooked Tomato Sauce (see page 39), *or* Mexican Green Tomato Sauce (see page 40)
1 medium onion, finely chopped

The tortillas A blender A mixing bowl	Break the tortillas into small pieces and blend until they are reduced to a coarse, flourlike (not pulverized) consistency. Transfer to a mixing bowl.
A blender 3 fresh Anaheim or California chilies, peeled (see page 30), or 1 four-ounce can peeled green chilies ⅔ cup hot milk	Blend the chilies, with their seeds, and the milk until smooth.
¾ teaspoon salt 1 tablespoon melted lard ¼ cup milk, approximately, if necessary	Add the chili mixture, salt, and lard to the ground tortillas and knead the mixture well. Set aside, covered, for at least 2 hours, to soften. Knead well again, then divide the dough into 12 equal portions. If the dough is crumbly, then add about ¼ cup more milk. Roll the dough into balls—they should be about 1½ inches in diameter. Flatten them to form small cakes about 2 inches in diameter and ¼ inch thick.
A frying pan Melted lard or peanut or safflower oil to a depth of ¼ inch Paper toweling The sour cream or sauce The chopped onion	Heat the oil over a high flame until it smokes, then lower the flame and let it cool off a little. Fry the cakes gently, a few at a time, for about 3 to 5 minutes on each side. (Take care that the fat is not too hot or there will be a crust on the outside of the *gordas* and they will be soggy inside—nor should it be too cool, or the *masa* will absorb too much of the oil.) Drain

well and serve, garnished with the sour cream or sauce and onion.

For a change you could always top the *gordas* with some shredded chicken and lettuce, or cheese and lettuce and a little sour cream.

Potato and Masa Gordas

6 SERVINGS

Have ready:

  1 medium onion, finely chopped
1½ cups finely shredded lettuce
and
  2 *chorizos*, crumbled and fried
  1 cup crumbled, well-salted farmer cheese (about 6 ounces)
or
  4 *chiles poblanos*, peeled (see page 30) and cut into strips, or canned, peeled green chilies, seeded and cut into strips
¾ cup Prepared Sour Cream (see page 27)

A large mixing bowl
1½ cups *masa harina* (see note below)
  6 tablespoons finely grated Romano or Sardo cheese
¾ teaspoon baking powder
1½ teaspoon salt, or to taste

Mix the dry ingredients together.

  1 cup cold water, approximately
  4 small potatoes (about ¾ pound), cooked, peeled and mashed

Add the water and mashed potatoes and knead the dough well. It should be smooth, not too dry (you may need to add a little more water), and just hold its shape when formed into the patties.

A lightly greased griddle or heavy frying pan

Heat the griddle or frying pan over a medium flame. Divide the dough into 12 equal parts; roll into balls about 1¾ inches in diameter and flatten them to make patties about 3½ inches in diameter and ⅜ inch thick. Cook the cakes for about 2 minutes on the first side, then turn them over, and while they cook on the second side—for about 2 minutes —pinch up a small ridge around the edge of each one.

A frying pan
Peanut or safflower oil to a depth of ½ inch
Paper toweling
The garnish (see above)

Heat the oil and fry the cakes lightly on either side. Drain, then garnish with the onion and lettuce and either the *chorizos* and farmer cheese or the chili strips and sour cream. Serve.

Prepared *masa* can be used with good results. If you do so, use ¾ pound and mix with the potatoes and dry ingredients and omit the water and *masa harina*.

The *gordas* will hold for a short time in a low oven, but soon become leathery. You can also cook the *gordas* on the griddle some time ahead and then fry them at the last moment.

They could be garnished with practically any leftovers you have around— shredded meat or chicken—or just sour cream and onion.

In Mexico *queso ranchero* or *fresco* would be used.

"Pot Tacos"

6 SERVINGS

Names can be confusing. If there were no chili in the dough these "tacos" would be known as *quesadillas*. There are actually three stages to the cooking: you can do all three or you could just as well just fry them and leave out the other two stages. Try and see what you prefer.

Have ready:

½ pound farmer cheese, crumbled and well-salted (about 1½ cups)
 2 *chiles poblanos*, peeled and cleaned and cut into strips (see page 30) or 3 canned, peeled green chilies, seeded and cut into narrow strips
 1 medium onion, finely chopped
 6 tablespoons finely grated Sardo cheese

A small bowl
  2 *chiles anchos,*
    toasted and cleaned
    (see page 30)
Hot water to cover
A blender
  ¾ cup water, approximately

Cover the chilies with hot water and leave them to soak for about 20 minutes, then drain and transfer to the blender jar. Add the water and blend until smooth.

A mixing bowl
1¼ cups Quaker *masa harina*
  ½ teaspoon salt
A lightly greased griddle or heavy frying pan

Combine the masa harina and salt, add the chili puree, and mix to a soft dough. (You may need a little more water.) Divide the dough into 12 equal parts and roll each part into a ball about 1¼ to 1½ inches in diameter. Meanwhile heat the griddle or frying pan.

A tortilla press
  2 small polyethylene bags

The farmer cheese
The chili strips

The heated griddle or frying pan

Press out a ball of the dough (see page 36) to make a tortilla about 3½ inches across. Peel off the top bag. Lift up the bottom bag and place it flat on your hand, with the dough on the palm. Put a little of the cheese and chili strips onto one half of the dough—not too near the edge. Lift the bag up and over so that the other half of the dough doubles over and covers the filling. Press the edges of the dough gently together and then carefully peel the bag from the "turnover." Cook for about 2 minutes on each side (the dough should be slightly speckled with brown and opaque).

A frying pan
Melted lard or oil
Paper toweling
A steamer
The chopped onion
The grated cheese

Heat the lard and fry the tacos lightly on both sides. Drain well. Transfer them to the steamer (see note on improvised steamers, page 33) and steam for a few minutes before serving them, garnished with the chopped onion and grated cheese.

These "tacos" should be eaten as soon as they are cooked. If they stand they become leathery. They can be formed ahead of time, ready for cooking, but kept under a slightly damp cloth of polyethylene wrap so that they do not dry out.

In Mexico *queso fresco* would be used inside, and *queso añejo* or *queso ranchero seco* for the garnish.

Quesadillas

4 TO 6 SERVINGS

Quesadillas are one of the Mexicans' favorite simple snacks. They are, in fact, uncooked tortillas stuffed with one of various fillings and folded over to make a "turnover." They are then toasted on a hot griddle or fried until golden. In many parts of Mexico they are just filled with strips of Chihuahua cheese, which melts and "strings" nicely—a Mexican requirement. I think it would be fair to say that the farther south one goes the more complicated they become. For instance, in central Mexico the simplest ones are filled with some of the braided Oaxaca cheese, a few fresh leaves of *epazote* and strips of peeled *chile poblano*. Potato and *chorizo* filling—that used for *tacos* (see p. 58)—is also a favorite version, while the most highly esteemed of all are those of sautéed squash blossoms (*flor de calabaza*) or the ambrosial fungus that grows on the corn (*huitlacoche*), both of which are at their best during the rainy months of summer and early fall. (These recipes are not within the scope of this book, but can be found in *The Cuisines of Mexico*). I remember one of our maids making them with cooked potato peelings and a few *epazote* leaves—they were delicious.

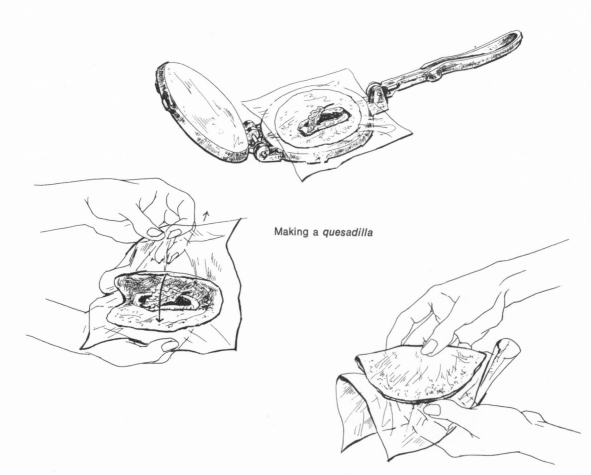

Making a *quesadilla*

Have ready:

The filling (see note above)

Preheat a lightly greased griddle.

A mixing bowl
1½ cups Quaker *masa harina*
¾ cup warm water, approximately

Mix the *masa harina* and water to a soft dough. Divide the dough into 12 equal parts and roll into balls about 1½ inches in diameter.

A tortilla press
  2 small polyethylene bags
The filling

The preheated griddle

Using the tortilla press and the bags, press out a ball of the dough (see page 34) to make a tortilla about 3½ to 4 inches in diameter. Peel off the top bag. Lift up the bottom bag and place it flat on your hand, with the dough on the palm. Put a little of the filling onto one half of the dough—not too near the edge. Bring the bag up and over so that the other half of the dough doubles over and covers the filling. Press the edges of the dough gently together and then gently peel the bag from the "turnover." Place it onto the griddle and cook for about 3 to 4 minutes on each side, then stand it up so that the u-shaped fold is also cooked. (Take care that the griddle is not too hot or the dough will be burned on the outside without cooking through sufficiently; it should be thoroughly opaque and speckled with brown.)

Or cook them as follows:

A frying pan
Melted lard or peanut or safflower oil to a depth of ½ inch
Paper toweling

Heat the lard and fry the *quesadillas* for 2 to 3 minutes on each side, or until they are golden brown but not too dry and crisp. Drain and serve immediately.

Quesadillas should be served immediately after they are cooked or they will soon become leathery. They could be formed ahead of time and kept wrapped in a slightly damp cloth or a piece of polyethylene wrap so that they do not dry out.

Sopes from Guadalajara

6 SERVINGS

Have ready:

1 cup Refried Beans (pinto or pink) (see page 18)
4 large *chiles poblanos*, peeled and cleaned (see page 30) or 5 canned
    peeled green chilies (a seven-ounce can), seeded and cut into strips
1 cup Uncooked Tomato Sauce (see page 41)
¾ cup crumbled, well-salted farmer cheese (about 4 ounces)
1 cup shredded lettuce

A blender
  2 *chiles anchos,*
    toasted and cleaned
    (see page 30)
1½ cups boiling water
  2 cloves garlic, peeled

Put the cleaned chilies into the blender jar, cover with the water and leave to soak for about 20 minutes (see note below). Add the garlic and blend until smooth.

A large mixing bowl
2½ cups *masa harina* or
    1¾ pounds pre-
    pared *masa*
  ¼ teaspoon salt
  6 tablespoons finely
    grated Sardo cheese
  ½ teaspoon baking
    powder
  ½ cup cold water
    approximately

Mix all the dry ingredients together, then add the chili puree and knead the masa well, working in the rest of the water—the dough should be soft but manageable. If you have time, set the masa aside to season for an hour—but do not refrigerate.

Divide the masa into 12 equal parts and roll into balls about 1¾ inches in diameter. Flatten each ball to make a thick tortilla about 3½ inches across and ¼ inch thick.

A lightly greased griddle

Heat the griddle and cook the *sopes* over a fairly low heat for about 3 minutes on one side, then turn them over and cook for another 3 minutes on the second side. While they are cooking on the second side, pinch up a small ridge around the edge of the dough on each. Remove a thin layer of the dough from the center, then flip each *sope* back onto the first side to cook the exposed raw dough lightly.

A frying pan
Melted lard or peanut
  or vegetable oil to
  a depth of ½ inch
Paper toweling
The garnish (see above)

Heat the lard and fry the sopes very lightly—30 seconds on each side (do not let them crust and brown). Drain well, then garnish with the beans first, then the chili strips, cheese, sauce, and lettuce.

If you are using prepared masa, drain most of the water from the soaked chilies before blending them.

You may want to cook the *sopes* on the griddle ahead of time and fry them at the last moment. They should be served as soon as possible after frying or they will become leathery.

In Mexico *queso añejo* would be put into the dough and *queso fresco* on top to garnish.

Tostaditas

4 SERVINGS

If you like playing about with dough, these are quite easy to make. They are a simplified version of the *panuchos* of Yucatán, crunchy and delicious.

Have ready:

1¼ cups cooked pinto or pink beans (see page 17)
  1 cup of the broth the beans were cooked in
Pickled Onion Rings (see page 43)
Strips of *chiles jalapeños en escabeche* (optional)

A small bowl
  4 *chiles anchos*,
    toasted and cleaned
    (see page 30)
Hot water to cover
A blender
The beans
The bean broth

Cover the chilies with hot water and let them soak for 15 to 20 minutes.

Drain the chilies, then transfer to the blender jar; add the beans and their broth and blend until almost smooth—there should be some texture to the puree.

A frying pan
  3 to 4 tablespoons
    melted lard or
    peanut or safflower
    oil

Heat the lard and cook the puree as for Refried Beans (see page 18). Set aside.

A mixing bowl
1¼ cups *masa harina*
  ¾ cup water, approximately
A tortilla press
  2 small polyethylene
    bags

Mix the *masa harina* and water to a soft dough. Divide the dough into 12 equal parts and roll into balls about 1¼ to 1½ inches in diameter. Using the tortilla press and the polyethylene bags, make tortillas (see page 36); they should be about 5″ across and puff up in the middle.

When they are cool enough to handle—but they must still be warm—make a "pocket" in each one by inserting the blade of a small pointed knife into the dough, near the edge of the tortilla, lifting up the thin layer of dough that puffed up when the tortilla was cooking. Take care not to pierce the underside of the tortilla. Stuff the pocket with a large spoonful of the bean paste, then press the dough back down into place.

The bean paste

Making a pocket for a *panucho*

A frying pan
Melted lard or peanut or
   safflower oil to a
   depth of ¼ inch
Paper toweling
The pickled onion rings
The chili strips

Heat the lard and fry the *tostaditas* until they are crisp around the edges. Drain well, then garnish and serve immediately.

Everything could be prepared ahead of time and the frying done at the last moment. Bean paste can always be prepared ahead and frozen.

Enchiladas Tultecas

6 SERVINGS

Once again the name is misleading. These are not *enchiladas* in the accepted "cooking method" sense, so I have followed my rule for the cooking method divisions of the book and included them here, under "*masa* fantasies."

This is such a colorful and "abundant" dish, but you may begin to wonder as you read the recipe whether it is all worth so much trouble. I did at first—then one day I happened to have all the ingredients handy and somehow it just fell together. I shredded the chicken for the topping because I wanted to pick the *enchilada* up to eat it—knives and forks are somehow all wrong—and as I crunched my way through all those layers of different textures, some fresh and some cooked, I knew it had been worth it.

The original suggests that refried beans should be served with them. If you wish to do this, ½ pound pinto or pink beans, cooked and refried (see page 18) should be plenty for 6 servings, assuming that there are 2 *enchiladas* per serving.

Have ready:

1 cup diced, cooked *chayote* (see note below)
1 cup diced, cooked potato (about ½ pound)
6 warmed individual serving plates
2 cups shredded, dressed lettuce (see page 24)
Jellied pig's feet (see page 46)
1 cup cooked peas, warmed
¾ cup crumbled farmer cheese
6 radishes, thinly sliced
1 three-pound chicken, poached and the meat divided into 12 portions
Strips of *chiles jalapeños en escabeche*

(*continued*)

A blender
  2 *chiles anchos,*
    toasted and cleaned
    (see page 30)
1⅓ cups hot water

Put the chilies into the blender jar, cover with the hot water, and leave to soak for 20 minutes.

A frying pan
  2 *chorizos*
The *chayote*
The potato

Meanwhile, skin and crumble the *chorizos*, and then cook them over a low flame until the fat starts to render out. Add the cooked vegetables and let them brown lightly with the *chorizos*, turning them over from time to time. Remove from the heat and keep warm.

The chilies
A mixing bowl
1½ cups *masa harina* or
    ¾ pound prepared
    masa
  ½ teaspoon salt
A tortilla press
  2 small polyethylene
    bags

Blend the chilies until smooth with the water in which they were soaked (see note below). Mix the puree into the *masa harina*, add the salt, and knead the dough well. Divide the dough into 12 equal parts and roll each one into a ball about 1½ inches in diameter. Press out with the tortilla press to make tortillas about 5 inches across and cook in the usual way (see page 36).

A frying pan
Peanut or safflower oil or
    melted lard to a
    depth of ¼ inch
Paper toweling
The warmed serving
    plates
The *chorizo* vegetable
    mixture
The garnish (see above)

Fry the tortillas lightly on both sides (do not let them become too crisp). Drain, then place 2 tortillas on each plate and garnish with *chorizos* and vegetables, lettuce, pig's feet, peas, farmer cheese, radishes, chicken and chili strips.

These *enchiladas* are better served on individual plates rather than attempting to arrange them on a platter, only to have them collapse as you serve them.

If you are using prepared *masa*, drain most of the water from the soaked chilies before blending them.

Chayotes, sometimes called "vegetable pears," need no description for Mexican cooks. Here in the United States they are widely available, in the South and in the Southwest, wherever Mexican produce is available. In the eastern states they can easily be found in Caribbean markets. If you can't get it, use zucchini instead.

Chalupas

SERVES 6

The word *chalupa* means "small canoe," and the antojito of that name is oval, or boat shaped, and pinched around the edge and cooked in exactly the same way as Sopes from Guadalajara (see page 108).

Have ready:

Garnish of your choice

A mixing bowl
1½ cups Quaker *masa harina*
¾ cup warm water, approximately
A tortilla press
  2 small polyethylene bags

Preheat a lightly greased griddle or thick frying pan.

Mix the *masa harina* and water together as if you were making tortillas. Divide the dough into 12 equal parts and roll each one into a cylinder about 5 inches long and ½ inch wide. Place slantwise onto the tortilla press and push down the top; the dough should press out to an elongated oval shape. Cook as for *sopes* (see page 108) and garnish with any shredded meat, lettuce, sauces, or crumbled cheese—whatever you have on hand.

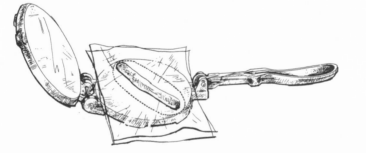

Making a *chalupa*

Enchiladas

I think the description above would certainly apply today to some of the commercial messes that are served up to us as *enchiladas*. But when ingredients are chosen with care and prepared with feeling, then a dish of *enchiladas* can provide an earthy and satisfying meal.

The variety is tremendous in Mexico, and I have tried to choose some of the most interesting recipes from regional cookbooks. They are grouped, as are nearly all the recipes in this book, by cooking methods rather than by names, which can be misleading.

GENERAL NOTES ON ENCHILADAS

There are two usual methods for making enchiladas: (1) the tortillas are "wilted" in hot fat, dipped into a cooked sauce, filled and rolled; and (2) the tortillas are dipped into a sauce—usually uncooked—and then fried and filled.

Preparing a dish of *enchiladas* can be rather a messy business, especially the first time, but it will soon come very easily. One of the main things to remember is to try and work fast so that the *enchiladas* do not become soggy in the process, or become cold and have to be reheated longer than is good for them. It will help if you can remember the following:

1. Have the filling and garnish all ready.

2. Be sure to put the filling on the *face* of the tortilla (see page 37). If you do not do this, your *enchiladas* will look ragged and possibly lose their chili coating on the outside.

3. The sauce can be made well ahead, if possible; in many cases it can be made and frozen.

4. Have a serving dish warming in the oven.

5. Prepare a tray with several layers of paper toweling.

6. Work with a pair of tongs—the ordinary kitchen type that do not have serrated or fluted ends, which tend to tear the tortillas—and a large spatula in the other hand to help control the tortilla. It is then much less likely to tear as you are frying it. I recommend a large, flat spatula with small, round perforations; the slotted type picks up and retains too much of the fat when you are frying the *enchiladas*.

6. Protect your clothes and hair from the splatter—a shower cap looks very funny, but it is the most practical thing to wear.

Enchiladas, like so many other quickly cooked Mexican dishes, are best served as soon as they are made, unless the recipe indicates otherwise. They will hold for no more than 15 minutes in a 350-degree oven if they are covered loosely with foil. They should be covered so that they do not dry out, and loosely, so that the steam that forms under the foil does not make them soggy.

The recipes call for what may seem to be rather a large amount of salt, but they do really need it. Don't forget that the tortillas are not salted.

Method 1

1. The tortillas used should not be too fresh and warm or they will absorb too much fat and probably tear or fall apart in the frying stage. Nor should they be too stale, or they will not wilt sufficiently in the fat and therefore not be pliable

enough to be rolled neatly. They should preferably have been made a few hours ahead and kept at room temperature covered with a cloth. This will prevent them from drying out. You may use frozen tortillas. Open the package and let them partially defrost—just enough to be able to separate them—which takes about 15 to 20 minutes. The fat will splatter when you first put them in and they will need a slightly longer frying time so that they soften and heat through sufficiently. Completely defrosted tortillas can also be used perfectly well.

2. There should be about ¼ inch of oil in the pan. Heat the oil to smoking point, then lower the flame and immerse the tortilla, turning it over once. It should be thoroughly heated through and quite limp. If the fat is not hot enough, then the tortilla will absorb too much and become greasy. If it is *too* hot, the edges of the tortilla will become crisp and it will be impossible to roll neatly.

3. Always drain the tortillas of any excess fat on paper toweling.

4. I find it easier to fry and drain *all* the tortillas before attempting to fill them. But work fast and keep them as warm as possible.

5. Mexican instructions always say, "Immerse the tortillas in the sauce, fill, and roll," but if you are not experienced in handling them, the tortillas may tear in the hot sauce. You may find it easier to spread about 2 tablespoons of the sauce over the face of the fried tortilla, then put some of the filling across it and roll it up fairly loosely. When they are all placed side by side on the heated dish, reheat the remaining sauce (never pour on the rest of the sauce or garnish until the dish is about to be served or it will become very soggy) and pour it over the *enchiladas* so that they are completely covered. If you find that the sauce needs diluting a little, then add a little broth or water.

6. See the general note on holding (page 115).

Swiss Chard Enchiladas

Have ready:

12 tortillas
A warmed ovenproof serving dish (ideally 8½ × 13 × 2)
¾ cup grated mild Cheddar, Muenster, or jack cheese
1 medium onion, finely chopped

1½ pounds Swiss chard
A large saucepan
   1 teaspoon salt, or to
     taste
	Wash the chard carefully, as it is inclined to be sandy at the base of the stalks. Put about 2 inches of water into the pan and bring it to a boil. Add the chard and salt and let it cook quickly over a high flame for about 5 minutes, turning it once so that it cooks evenly. Drain and chop; it should be *al dente*.

A frying pan
   3 tablespoons peanut
     or safflower oil
   2 cloves garlic, peeled
     and chopped
	Heat the oil and fry the garlic gently for about 2 minutes. Add the chard and cook for another 3 minutes. Adjust the seasoning and set aside in a warm place.

A blender
   2 medium tomatoes
     (¾ pound), broiled
     (see page 29), or
     1½ cups canned,
     drained
   1 clove garlic
  ¼ medium onion
   2 canned *chiles
     chipotles*
	Blend the tomatoes with the rest of the ingredients until smooth.

A frying pan
   2 tablespoons peanut
     or safflower oil
   1 teaspoon salt, or to
     taste
  ¼ teaspoon granulated
     sugar
  ⅔ cups broth or water
	Heat the oil and add the sauce, sugar and salt (less if broth is used) to the pan and cook over a fairly high flame, stirring it almost constantly, until it has reduced—about 5 minutes. Add the broth and bring to a boil, then remove from the heat and keep warm.
	
	Preheat the broiler.

(continued)

A frying pan
The tortillas
Peanut or safflower oil to
a depth of ¼ inch
Paper toweling
The tomato sauce
The Swiss chard filling
¾ cup sour cream,
commercial or
homemade (see
page 27)
The warmed serving dish
Broth as necessary
The grated cheese
The chopped onion

Heat the oil and fry the tortillas, one by one, briefly. Drain well and keep warm, then immerse them, one by one, in the sauce. Put some of the filling across each tortilla, along with a little of the sour cream, then roll up and put side by side in the dish. If necessary, dilute the sauce with a little more broth and pour it over the *enchiladas*. Sprinkle with the cheese and run under a hot broiler to melt it, then sprinkle with the onion and serve.

The chilies are fiery hot, so use them with discretion. In Mexico the whole dried *chipotles* would be used. They should be soaked in hot water for about 20 minutes before blending with the tomatoes. *Queso fresco* would be used traditionally, but Chihuahua is extremely good, too.

Enchiladas from Fresnillo

4 TO 6 SERVINGS

Have ready:

12 tortillas
A warmed ovenproof serving dish (ideally 9 × 13½ × 2)
½ pound farmer cheese (about 1½ cups), crumbled and well salted
1 medium onion, finely chopped
1 avocado, thinly sliced (see page 16)
6 large radishes, thinly sliced
¾ cup Prepared Sour Cream (see page 27)
2 *chorizos*, crumbled and fried

A small bowl
3 *chiles anchos*,
toasted and cleaned
Hot water to cover
A blender
¼-inch piece cinnamon
bark
1 clove

Cover the chilies with hot water and leave them to soak for about 20 minutes. Drain, then transfer the chilies to the blender jar, add the rest of the ingredients, and blend until smooth.

(*continued*)

⅛ teaspoon dried
   oregano
⅛ teaspoon dried
   thyme
⅛ teaspoon dried
   marjoram
 3 peppercorns
 1 tablespoon sesame
   seeds, toasted (see
   page 27)
 ¼ cup shelled peanuts,
   fried
1½ cups cold water
 ¾ teaspoon salt, or to
   taste

A frying pan
   **2 tablespoons peanut
      or safflower oil**

Heat the oil and cook the sauce over a me-dium flame for about 8 minutes, stirring and scraping the bottom of the pan almost con-stantly. Remove from the flame and keep warm.

**Peanut or safflower oil to
   a depth of ¼ inch**
The tortillas
Paper toweling

Fry the tortillas, one by one, lightly on both sides. Drain well and keep them warm while you do the rest.

The sauce
The farmer cheese
The chopped onion
The warmed serving dish
Water as necessary
The garnish (see above)

Dip the tortillas into the sauce, then fill each one with some of the cheese and onion. Roll up loosely and place side by side in the serv-ing dish. Add a little water to the remaining sauce, then bring to a boil and pour over the *enchiladas*. Garnish with the avocado slices, sliced onion, sour cream, and *chorizos* and serve immediately.

In Mexico *queso añejo* or *fresco* would be used.

Red Enchiladas (*from Aguascalientes*)

4 TO 6 SERVINGS

Have ready:

A warmed serving dish (13½ × 9 × 2)
 12 tortillas
 ½ pound farmer cheese (about 1½ cups)
 1 medium onion, finely chopped
 1 hard-boiled egg white, finely chopped
1½ cups finely shredded lettuce
 6 radishes, thinly sliced
Strips of *chiles jalapeños en escabeche*

A blender
 4 *chiles anchos,*
    toasted and cleaned
    (see page 30)
1½ cups hot milk
 1 teaspoon salt, or to
    taste
 1 clove garlic, peeled
 1 hard-boiled egg yolk

Put the chilies in the blender jar with the milk and leave to soak for about 20 minutes. Add the rest of the ingredients and blend until smooth. (You will have about 2 cups of sauce; add water if necessary to make up that quantity.)

A frying pan
 2 tablespoons peanut
    or safflower oil

Heat the oil, add the sauce, and cook for about 5 minutes over a medium heat, stirring and scraping sides and bottom of pan all the time. Remove from heat and keep warm.

A frying pan
Peanut or safflower oil to
    a depth of ¼ inch
The tortillas
Paper toweling

Heat the oil and fry the tortillas, one by one, briefly on both sides. Drain well and keep warm.

The sauce
The farmer cheese
The chopped onion
The warmed serving dish
A little hot water or
    broth, if necessary
The garnish (see above)

Dip the tortillas, one by one, into the sauce. Fill each one with some of the cheese and onion, then roll and place side by side in the serving dish. Dilute the remaining sauce, if necessary and pour it over the *enchiladas*. Garnish with the chopped egg whites, the lettuce, sliced radishes, and chili strips and serve immediately.

Green Enchiladas (*from Aguascalientes*)

4 TO 6 SERVINGS

Have ready:

A warmed serving dish (9 × 13½ × 2)
 12 tortillas
1½ to 2 cups cooked, shredded, and well-salted chicken (see page 56)
1½ cups finely shredded, dressed lettuce (see page 24)
   6 large radishes, thinly sliced
  ½ cup pitted, halved green olives

A blender
   3 *chiles poblanos*,
      peeled and seeded
      (see page 30), or
      5 canned, peeled
      green chilies
   2 large romaine
      lettuce leaves
   1 clove
  ½ cup chicken broth

Blend the chilies together with the rest of the ingredients until very smooth.

A frying pan
   2 tablespoons oil
  ½ teaspoon salt, or to
      taste
  ½ cup sour cream,
      commercial or
      homemade
  ½ cup chicken broth

Heat the oil and cook the sauce over a fairly high flame for about 5 minutes, stirring and scraping the bottom of the pan almost constantly. Add the rest of the ingredients and just heat through, then remove from the heat and keep warm.

A frying pan
Peanut or safflower oil to
      a depth of ¼ inch
The tortillas
Paper toweling

Heat the oil and fry the tortillas, one at a time, briefly on both sides. Drain well and keep warm.

The sauce
The chicken
The warmed serving dish
The garnish (see above)

Dip the tortillas, one by one, into the sauce, then fill each one with some of the chicken. Roll up and place side by side on the warmed dish. Pour the remaining sauce over the *enchiladas*, garnish with the lettuce, sliced radishes, and olives and serve immediately.

Enchiladas from Zacatecas

4 TO 6 SERVINGS

For those who like their *enchiladas* strong and pungent, this is the dish. And although it's not in the original recipe, I like to serve *chiles jalapeños en escabeche* with them, as their acidity makes such a good foil for the chili sauce.

Have ready:

12 tortillas
A warmed serving dish (ideally 9 × 13½ × 2)
1½ cups well salted farmer cheese (about ½ pound)
 1 medium onion, finely chopped

A frying pan
  3 *chorizos*
  2 medium potatoes, cooked until barely tender and cubed

Skin and crumble the *chorizos* and put them to cook over a low flame. When the fat begins to render out, add the potatoes and fry together, stirring from time to time until just beginning to brown. Remove from the heat and keep warm.

A small bowl
  5 *chiles anchos*, toasted and cleaned (see page 30)
Hot water to cover
A blender
  3 large romaine lettuce leaves
  5 peppercorns
  3 cloves garlic, peeled
  1 teaspoon salt
  ¾ cup water

Cover the chilies with hot water and leave to soak for about 20 minutes. Drain, then transfer the chilies to the blender jar and blend until smooth with the rest of the ingredients.

A frying pan
  3 tablespoons peanut or safflower oil or lard
  1 tablespoon all-purpose flour

Heat the oil, then add the flour and cook it until it is a pale golden brown. Add the blended ingredients and cook the sauce over a medium flame for about 5 to 7 minutes, stirring and scraping the bottom of the pan constantly.

  ⅔ cup hot broth or water, approximately

Add the broth and grated avocado pit and bring to a boil; the sauce will be thick. Remove from the heat and keep warm.

1½ teaspoons grated
    avocado pit (see
    page 15)

A frying pan	Heat the oil and fry the tortillas, one by one, briefly on both sides. Drain well and keep warm.
Peanut or safflower oil to a depth of ½ inch	
The tortillas	
Paper toweling	

The sauce	Dip the tortillas, one by one, into the sauce. Put a little of the cheese and onion onto each one, then roll up loosely and place side by side in the warmed dish. Pour the remaining sauce over the *enchiladas*, garnish with the *chorizo*-potato mixture, and serve.
The farmer cheese	
The chopped onion	
The warmed serving dish	
The *chorizo*-potato mixture	

In Mexico *queso añejo* would be used.

Chili and Egg Enchiladas

4 TO 6 SERVINGS

This makes a substantial dish of *enchiladas;* the chili-egg sauce is both savory and satisfying.

Have ready:

12 tortillas
A warmed serving dish (ideally 9 × 13½ × 2)
  1 medium onion, finely chopped
  6 heaped tablespoons finely grated Romano or Sardo cheese

A bowl	Cover the chilies with hot water and leave to soak for about 20 minutes. Drain, reserving 1½ cups of the soaking water.
5 *chiles pasillas*, toasted and cleaned (see page 30)	
4 *chiles anchos*, toasted and cleaned (see page 30)	
Hot water to cover	

(continued)

A blender
 1 clove garlic, peeled
⅓ medium onion
 1 teaspoon salt, or to
   taste

Add the chilies, together with the reserved soaking water and the rest of the ingredients, to the blender jar and blend until smooth.

A frying pan
 3 tablespoons peanut
   or safflower oil

Heat the oil and fry the sauce over a medium flame for about 5 minutes, stirring and scraping the bottom of the pan almost constantly.

 3 very large eggs
 1 cup hot broth or
   water

Beat the eggs well and add them, along with the broth, to the mixture in the pan. Cook over a medium flame, stirring constantly, until the eggs are set and the sauce thickened—5 to 8 minutes. Set aside and keep warm.

A frying pan
Peanut or safflower oil to
   a depth of ¼ inch
The tortillas
Paper toweling

Heat the oil and fry the tortillas, one by one, briefly on both sides. Drain well and keep warm.

The chili-egg mixture
The warmed serving dish
The chopped onion
The grated cheese

Dip each tortilla into the chili-egg mixture, double over, and set in the warmed dish. Pour the remaining sauce over the *enchiladas*, garnish with the onion and cheese, and serve.

Since the egg is scrambled in the sauce, the sauce will have a rough texture.

Enchiladas from Yucatán

4 TO 6 SERVINGS

Have ready:

12 tortillas
 6 large eggs, hard boiled, finely chopped, and well salted
 1 medium onion, finely chopped
A warmed serving dish (ideally 9 × 13½ × 2)
 6 large radishes, thinly sliced or cut into flowers (see page 26)
¾ cup crumbled, well salted farmer cheese (about 4 ounces)

A small bowl
 3 *chiles anchos*, toasted
   and cleaned (see
   page 30)
¼ medium onion,
   roughly chopped
 1 large clove garlic,
   peeled and roughly
   chopped
 1 tomato (about 6
   ounces), broiled
   (see page 29) or ¾
   cup canned, drained
   tomatoes
¾ cup water
¾ teaspoon salt, or to
   taste

Cover the chilies with hot water and leave to soak for about 20 minutes, then drain and blend, together with the rest of the ingredients, until smooth.

A frying pan
 2 tablespoons peanut
   or safflower oil

Heat the oil, then add the sauce and cook it over a fairly high flame for about 5 minutes, stirring and scraping the bottom of the pan almost constantly. Remove from the heat and keep warm.

A frying pan
Peanut or safflower oil to
   a depth of ¼ inch

Heat the oil and fry the tortillas, one by one, lightly on each side. Drain well and keep warm.

The tortillas
Paper toweling
The sauce
The chopped hard-
   boiled egg
The chopped onion
The warmed serving dish
The radishes
The farmer cheese

Dip the tortillas, one by one, into the sauce, then fill each one with a little of the egg and onion, roll up, and put side by side in the warmed dish. Garnish with the radishes and cheese and serve immediately.

In Mexico *queso fresco* would be used.

Green Enchiladas (*from San Luis Potosí*)

4 TO 6 SERVINGS

Have ready:

12 tortillas
A warmed ovenproof serving dish (8½ × 13 × 2)
1½ to 2 cups cooked, shredded, and well-salted chicken (see page 56)
  1 medium onion, finely chopped
  ½ cup Prepared Sour Cream (see page 27)
  2 ounces farmer cheese (about ½ cup), crumbled and well salted

2 cups cooked fresh or canned, drained Mexican green tomatoes (see page 25)	Blend the green tomatoes with the rest of the ingredients until smooth.
¼ teaspoon granulated sugar (if the canned green tomatoes are used)	
4 *chiles serranos* or any small, hot green chilies	
3 sprigs coriander, leaves only	
⅓ cup milk	
1 clove garlic, peeled	
1 teaspoon salt	
A frying pan 2 tablespoons peanut or safflower oil 2 tablespoons sour cream, commercial or homemade (see page 27)	Heat the oil. Cook the sauce over a fairly high flame until reduced and seasoned—about 5 minutes. Remove from the heat, add the sour cream, and set aside. Keep warm.
A frying pan Peanut or safflower oil to a depth of ¼ inch The tortillas Paper toweling	Heat the oil and fry the tortillas, one by one, briefly on each side. Drain well and keep warm.

The green sauce
The shredded chicken
The warmed serving dish
A little water or broth
The garnish (see above)

Dip the tortillas, one by one, into the sauce. Fill each one with some of the chicken, then roll and place side by side in the warmed dish. Dilute the rest of the sauce, if necessary, and pour it over the *enchiladas*. Garnish with the onion, cheese, and sour cream and serve immediately.

In Mexico *queso fresco* would be used.

Enfrijoladas

4 TO 6 SERVINGS

The name *enfrijoladas* means that the tortillas are immersed in a puree of beans, an appropriate and succinct translation. It is traditional to fold tortillas for *enfrijoladas* into fours, but it is easier and less messy just to fold them over.

Have ready:

12 tortillas
A warmed serving dish (about 9½ × 13½ × 2)
½ pound cooked pinto beans (about 2½ cups) (see page 17)
 1 cup Mexican Green Tomato Sauce (see page 40)
 5 *chorizos*, cooked (see page 22)
 1 medium onion, finely chopped
½ cup crumbled farmer cheese (about 3 ounces)
 2 tablespoons roughly chopped coriander leaves

A blender
 2 avocado leaves,
     toasted lightly (see
     page 16) (optional)
The cooked beans
Water as necessary

Put the avocado leaves into the blender jar with the beans. Blend until smooth, adding enough water to make 3 cups puree.

A frying pan
 2 tablespoons melted
     lard
Salt as necessary

Heat the lard and fry the puree for about 3 minutes, stirring it all the time. Adjust the seasoning, then set aside and keep warm.

(*continued*)

A frying pan
Peanut or safflower oil
    to a depth of ¼ inch
The tortillas
Paper toweling

Heat the oil and cook the tortillas, one by one, briefly on both sides. Drain well and keep warm.

The bean puree
The *chorizos*
The Mexican green
    tomato sauce
The warmed serving dish
A little hot water, if
    necessary
The garnish (see above)

Spread a thin coating of the bean puree across the face of each tortilla, then spread on some of the *chorizos* and about 2 tablespoons of the sauce and double the tortilla over. Set them, overlapping slightly, into the warmed dish. Dilute the rest of the bean puree, if necessary, and pour it over the tortillas. Garnish with the chopped onion, farmer cheese, and coriander leaves and serve immediately.

This is, as with all *enchilada* dishes, best eaten as soon as it is prepared. The filling and sauce could be done ahead of time and the dish assembled at the last moment.

It is far better to cook the beans a day ahead, since the flavor improves so much. As they stand the beans absorb the liquid, so you may have to add about ½ cup to make up the 3 cups of puree—and in any case, to allow the blender blades to work properly.

Pork with Green Enchiladas

6 SERVINGS

Have ready:

12 tortillas
A large warmed serving platter
  6 large radish flowers (see page 26)
  2 cups shredded, lightly dressed lettuce (see page 24)

THE MEAT

A large frying pan or
    flameproof baking
    dish
  3 pounds country-style
    spareribs
Water to barely cover

Put the meat into a pan just large enough to take in one layer, if possible. Barely cover the meat with water (see note below), add the garlic and salt, and bring to a boil. Lower the heat to medium and let the meat cook until it is tender, the water evaporated, and the

2 cloves garlic, peeled
and crushed
1½ teaspoons salt

fat rendered out. Let the meat fry in its fat, turning it from time to time until it is well browned—about 1 hour. Set aside and keep warm.

THE SAUCE

A frying pan
2 tablespoons peanut
or safflower oil
½ medium onion,
finely chopped

Heat the oil and fry the onion gently until soft, not brown.

A blender
1 cup cooked fresh or
canned Mexican
green tomatoes (if
canned, drained and
blended with ½ cup
water and a pinch of
sugar) (see page 25)
2 large romaine let-
tuce leaves
2 sprigs *epazote*,
leaves only
2 cloves garlic, peeled
¾ teaspoon salt
¼ cup broth or water
2 *chiles poblanos*,
peeled and cleaned
(see page 30), or 2
canned, peeled
green chilies
6 sprigs coriander,
leaves only

Blend the ingredients until smooth. Add to the onion in the pan and fry over a fairly high flame, stirring and scraping the bottom of the pan until it has reduced a little and is well seasoned (about 5 minutes). Remove from the heat and keep warm.

THE FILLING

A frying pan
2 tablespoons peanut
or safflower oil
1 tablespoon butter

Heat the butter and oil together.

5 eggs
½ teaspoon salt
⅔ medium onion, finely
   chopped

Meanwhile, beat the eggs together well, then add the salt and the onion. Pour into the hot fat and scramble them over a very low flame; they should be just set and tender. Remove from the heat and keep warm.

THE TORTILLAS

A frying pan
Peanut or safflower oil
   to a depth of ¼ inch
Paper toweling

Heat the oil and fry the tortillas, one by one, lightly on both sides. Drain and keep warm.

THE ASSEMBLY

The sauce
The filling
The warmed serving
   platter
A little water, if necessary
The cooked pork
The radish flowers
The lettuce

Dip the tortillas into the sauce, fill each one with some of the egg mixture, then roll up and place them on the serving dish. Dilute the remaining sauce, if necessary, and pour over the *enchiladas*. Place the pork around them, garnish the dish, and serve immediately.

The sauce can, of course, be done ahead of time. The pork could be done about 1 hour ahead, but would have to be kept tightly covered and heated through gently.

It is better to put less water with the meat than too much; you can always add some if the water has evaporated and the meat is still not tender enough. If you put in too much, then the meat will fall apart by the time the frying stage is reached.

Method 2

1. The tortillas used should neither be too fresh and warm—they will become soggy when immersed in the uncooked sauce—nor should they be too stale, or the sauce will not adhere and coat them sufficiently well and they will not wilt in the hot fat. Partially frozen tortillas cannot, obviously, be used, but defrosted ones are quite satisfactory. Best are those that have been made several hours ahead, covered with a cloth to prevent drying, and left at room temperature.

2. There should be about ¼ inch of oil in the pan. Heat the oil to the smoking point, then lower the flame and let it cool off a little before attempting to fry the *enchiladas;* sauces made with dried chilies burn very quickly. Dip a tortilla into the prepared sauce and fry for about one minute on each side, remembering that not only must the tortilla be thoroughly heated through, but the raw ingredients in the sauce cooked sufficiently. Do not let the edges of the tortilla become crisp or it will be impossible to roll. Drain on paper toweling.

3. Very often, if a chili sauce is thickened with cream and eggs, it will stick to the paper toweling and hardly any will remain on the tortilla itself: in that case, start draining them on a sheet of plastic wrap.

4. I find it easier and less messy to fry and drain all the *enchiladas* before attempting to fill them. Try to spread them out as much as you can and not stack them one on top of the other; they stick together very easily and become mushy with the heat of the others. But at the same time try to keep them as warm as possible. *Work fast.*

5. Put some of the filling across the *face* of each tortilla (see page 37), roll up fairly loosely, and place them side by side into a heated serving dish. Drain all but 2 tablespoons of the oil from the frying pan, reheat, and put in the remaining sauce (remember that it is uncooked). Dilute it with a little water or broth, bring to a boil, and let it cook fairly quickly, stirring all the time—or rather scraping the bottom of the pan so that it does not stick—for about 3 minutes. Pour the sauce over the *enchiladas;* garnish, and serve immediately.

6. (If you want to hold them for a short while, cover lightly with foil and set in a 350-degree oven.) When holding *enchiladas* in the oven, never put the sauce and garnish over them until ready to serve, unless recipe instructions say otherwise.

7. See also general notes, page 115.

Tomato Enchiladas

4 TO 6 SERVINGS

Have ready:

12 tortillas
1½ to 2 cups cooked, shredded, and well-salted chicken, warmed
A warmed serving dish (ideally 9 × 13 × 2)
  3 medium carrots (about ½ pound) cooked until barely tender and sliced
½ pound green beans, left whole and cooked until barely tender
Strips of canned *chiles jalapeños en escabeche*
⅔ cup Prepared Sour Cream (page 27)
½ cup crumbled, well-salted farmer cheese (about 3 ounces)

A saucepan
  1 pound tomatoes, skin left on, chopped
⅓ medium onion
⅛ teaspoon dried thyme
⅛ teaspoon dried oregano
¾ cup water
  1 teaspoon salt
  4 *chiles serranos* or any other fresh, hot green chilies
A blender

Put all the ingredients into the saucepan and simmer for about 15 minutes, then transfer to the blender jar and blend until smooth.

A frying pan
Peanut or safflower oil to a depth of ¼ inch
The tortillas
Paper toweling

Heat the oil. Dip the tortillas, one by one, into the sauce and fry them briefly on both sides in the oil. (Very little sauce seems to hang on to the tortilla, but it does flavor it well). Drain on the paper toweling. Set the pan and the oil aside.

Preheat the oven to 350 degrees.

The warmed shredded chicken
The warmed serving dish

Put a little of the shredded chicken across each tortilla, roll loosely and set side by side in the serving dish. Cover loosely and set in the oven while you prepare the garnish.

The reserved oil	In the same oil, fry the beans and carrots until
The carrots	they are just beginning to brown. Sprinkle
The beans	them over the *enchiladas*.
The remaining sauce	Reheat the remaining sauce and pour it over
The garnish (see above)	the *enchiladas*. Garnish with the chili strips,
	sour cream, and farmer cheese and serve immediately.

This sauce is so much better with fresh tomatoes, but if they are not available, then substitute 2½ cups canned, drained tomatoes and ⅓ cup water instead of ¾ cup.

In Mexico *queso fresco* would be used.

Entomatados

SERVES 4 TO 6

This is a surprisingly simple and good recipe from the north of Mexico, particularly appealing to those who do not like spicy food and to vegetarians. They are prepared in the same way as *enchiladas*.

Have ready:

  12 tortillas
   1 medium onion, finely chopped
   ½ pound farmer cheese (about 1½ cups), crumbled and well salted
A warmed ovenproof serving dish (about 9 × 13½ × 2)
   ½ cup grated Cheddar, Muenster, or similar cheese
   1 cup Prepared Sour Cream (see page 27)

A frying pan	Heat the oil and cook the onion gently until
2 tablespoons peanut or safflower oil	soft but not brown.
⅓ medium onion, finely chopped	
A blender	Blend the tomatoes until smooth, then add
1¼ pounds tomatoes, broiled (see page 29), or 2½ cups canned, drained	them, along with the salt, to the onions in the pan. Cook over a fairly high flame for about 4 minutes, stirring almost constantly. Remove from the heat and keep warm.
¾ teaspoon salt	

(continued)

A frying pan
Peanut or safflower oil
    to a depth of ¼ inch
The tortillas
Paper toweling

Heat the oil. Dip the tortillas, one by one, into the sauce—it should lightly coat them—and fry them for about 1 minute on each side in the oil. Drain well.

Preheat the oven to 375 degrees.

The chopped onion
The farmer cheese
The warmed serving dish
The grated cheese
The sour cream

Put a little of the onion and cheese across each tortilla, roll up, and place side by side in the serving dish. Sprinkle with the grated cheese, then set the dish, uncovered, into the oven for a few moments just to heat through. As the cheese begins to melt, pour the sour cream over and serve immediately.

If you find this too messy to prepare, and virtually no sauce hangs on the tortilla, then follow Method 1 (see page 115). However, the flavor and texture of the *entomatados* will not be quite as good.

Enchiladas from Juchipila

4 TO 6 SERVINGS

Have ready:

A warmed ovenproof serving dish (ideally 9 × 13½ × 2)
 12 tortillas
  ½ pound farmer cheese (about 1½ cups), crumbled and well salted
1½ medium onions, finely chopped
  6 tablespoons finely grated Sardo cheese
1½ cups finely shredded lettuce
  6 large radishes, thinly sliced

A small bowl
  4 *chiles anchos,*
    toasted and cleaned
    (see page 30)
Hot water to cover
A blender
  1 large tomato (about
    ½ pound), broiled
    (see page 29), or 1
    cup canned, drained

Cover the chilies with hot water and leave to soak for about 20 minutes, then drain and transfer to the blender jar. Blend with the rest of the ingredients until smooth.

(*continued*)

¼-inch piece cinnamon
    bark
1 clove
4 peppercorns
¾ teaspoon salt, or to
    taste
1 cup water

A frying pan
Peanut or safflower oil
    to a depth of ¼ inch
The tortillas
Paper toweling
The sauce

Dip the tortillas, one by one, into the sauce —it should coat them lightly—and fry for a minute or so on both sides. Drain and keep warm. Set the pan and the oil aside.

Preheat the oven to 350 degrees.

The farmer cheese
The chopped onion
The warmed serving dish

Fill each tortilla with a little of the cheese and onion, using two-thirds of the onion and setting the remainder aside, roll up loosely and set side by side in the warmed dish. Cover with foil and set in the oven to keep warm.

The reserved oil
The remaining sauce
The garnish (see above)

In 2 tablespoons of the same oil, fry the remaining sauce for a minute or so. Pour it over the *enchiladas*, sprinkle with the remaining chopped onions and grated cheese, and decorate the dish with the lettuce and radishes.

In Mexico *queso añejo* would be used.

Red Enchiladas (*from Jardín de San Marco*)

4 TO 6 SERVINGS

If you leave out the *chorizo*, this could become an attractive vegetarian dish.

Although the original recipe does not say so, I like to leave the vegetables for an hour or so in a weak vinegar-water solution so that they are slightly acidy and provide a good foil for the chili sauce. This is, in fact, quite often done in the central part of Mexico.

Have ready:

12 tortillas
½ pound farmer cheese (about 1½ cups), crumbled and well salted
1 medium onion, finely chopped
A warmed ovenproof serving dish (ideally 9 × 13½ × 2)
¾ cup cooked, diced carrot
¾ cup cooked, diced potato
¾ cup cooked, cut green beans
¾ cup cooked zucchini squash
6 tablespoons finely grated Romano cheese
Strips of *chiles jalapeños en escabeche*
Romaine lettuce leaves, left whole

A small bowl
  4 *chiles anchos*, toasted and cleaned (see page 30)
Hot water to cover
  5 peppercorns
¼-inch piece cinnamon bark
  1 clove
  1 large clove garlic, peeled
  1 teaspoon salt
  1 cup water, more if necessary

Cover the chilies with hot water and leave them to soak for about 20 minutes, then drain and transfer to the blender jar. Add the rest of the ingredients and blend until smooth. Add more water if necessary to make the sauce up to 2 cups, then set aside.

A frying pan
Peanut or safflower oil to a depth of ¼ inch
The tortillas
Paper toweling

Heat the oil. Dip the tortillas, one by one, into the sauce—it should just lightly coat them —and fry them briefly on both sides. Drain well. Set the pan and the oil aside.

Preheat the oven to 350 degrees.

The farmer cheese **The chopped onion** **The warmed serving dish**	Fill each tortilla with some of the cheese and onion, roll up loosely, and set them side by side in the warmed dish. Cover loosely with foil and set in the oven to keep warm while you prepare the garnish.

The reserved oil
 2 *chorizos*, **skinned
   and crumbled**
The cooked vegetables
   (see above)
An ovenproof dish
	In the same oil, fry the *chorizos* gently for a few minutes. Add the cooked vegetables and cook, stirring them from time to time, until they are well heated through. Remove from the pan, leaving the oil behind, and transfer to the ovenproof dish, and keep warm in the oven.

The reserved oil **The remaining sauce** **The vegetables** **The lettuce** **The chili strips** **The grated cheese**	In the same oil, fry the sauce over a high flame for a minute or so. Pour over the *enchiladas* and garnish with the vegetables. Sprinkle the cheese over the vegetables and decorate the dish with the chilies and lettuce leaves.

In Mexico *queso añejo* would be used inside the *enchiladas* and as a garnish, and *chiles bolas* used for decoration.

Enchiladas from San Luis Potosí

Have ready:

12 tortillas
A warmed serving dish (ideally 9 × 13½ × 2)
  6 large romaine lettuce leaves, dressed (see page 24)
  6 large radishes, thinly sliced
  6 tablespoons finely grated Sardo cheese
  1 medium onion, finely chopped

A frying pan
  4 *chorizos*
  1 pound red bliss or
      other waxy potatoes
      (skin included, if
      you like), cooked
      and cut into small
      dice

Skin and crumble the *chorizos* and cook over a low flame. When the fat begins to render out, add the potato pieces and fry, turning them over from time to time, until they are just beginning to brown—about 8 minutes. Cover, then remove from the heat and keep warm.

A blender
  3 *chiles anchos*, toasted
      and cleaned (see
      page 30)
¾ cup hot milk
¾ cup hot water
⅔ cup cooked fresh or
      canned Mexican
      green tomatoes (if
      canned, drained and
      blended with ⅓ cup
      water and a pinch
      of sugar)
½ cup crumbled farmer
      cheese (about 3
      ounces)
¾ teaspoon salt, or to
      taste
  1 egg
⅓ cup sour cream, com-
      mercial or home-
      made (see page 27)

Put the chilies in the blender jar, cover with the milk and water, and leave to soak for about 20 minutes. Add the rest of the ingredients to the chilies and blend until smooth.

A frying pan
Peanut or safflower oil
    to a depth of ½ inch
The tortillas
The sauce
Water, if necessary
Paper toweling or clear
    plastic wrap

Heat the oil—*do not let it become too hot, as this sauce burns quickly*—then dip the tortillas, one by one, into the sauce, which should coat it well (if the sauce is too thick, dilute it with a little water) and fry them for about a minute on each side. Drain well. (If you find that the enchiladas are sticking to the paper and losing the chili coating, then drain on the clear polyethylene wrap.)

The *chorizo*-potato
    filling
The warmed serving dish
The garnish (see above)

Put a little of the filling onto each tortilla, roll up, and set them side by side in the warmed dish. Garnish with the lettuce, sliced radishes, grated cheese, and chopped onion and serve.

In Mexico *queso añejo* would be used.
    This dish will not hold; the tortillas become too soggy.

"Enchiladas Tacos"

4 to 6 servings

Have ready:

  12 tortillas
   6 tablespoons finely grated Parmesan cheese
1½ cups shredded, lightly dressed lettuce (see page 24)
A warmed ovenproof serving dish (8½ × 13 × 2)

A frying pan
  2 tablespoons peanut
     or safflower oil
½ medium onion,
     finely chopped
½ pound lean ground
     pork
½ pound lean ground
     beef

Heat the oil and fry the onion gently until soft, then add the ground meats and cook gently, stirring from time to time, for about 10 minutes.

A blender
  1 cup canned to-
    matoes, drained, or
  1 large tomato
    (about ½ pound),
    broiled (see page
    29)
¾ teaspoon salt
Freshly ground pepper

Blend the tomatoes briefly, then add to the meats in the pan, season, and cook over a medium flame until the mixture is almost dry—about 8 to 10 minutes. Remove from the heat and keep warm.

A saucepan
  6 *chiles anchos* or
    New Mexican
    chilies (*chiles de
    ristra*), cleaned
    (see page 30)
1½ cups milk
A blender

Add the chilies to the saucepan, along with the milk. Bring to a boil and simmer for about 5 minutes, then remove from the heat and let soak for another 5 minutes. Blend until smooth, then set aside.

  2 large eggs
  1 teaspoon salt
The chili sauce

Separate the eggs. Beat the whites until stiff but not dry, then add the salt and yolks and mix well. Add the chili sauce to the mixture and stir in well.

The tortillas
A frying pan
Peanut or safflower oil
    to a depth of ½ inch
A tray covered with
    layers of paper
    towels

Dip the tortillas, one by one, into the sauce—they should be covered completely with a good, but not too thick, coating—and fry in the hot fat on both sides. Drain well and keep warm.

The filling
The warmed serving dish
The lettuce

Put a large spoonful of the filling across each tortilla. Roll up and place side by side in the serving dish. Garnish the dish with the lettuce and serve immediately.

This is a messy dish to prepare the first time. Be sure to read the notes on page 115.

Huastec Enchiladas

Have ready:

12 tortillas
A large warmed serving platter
   1 large onion, finely chopped
   6 tablespoons finely grated Romano cheese
   2 cups Refried Beans (pinto or pink) (see page 18), warmed
   1 large can sardines, seasoned with lemon juice and salt
   2 cups finely shredded, lightly dressed lettuce (see page 24)
Strips of canned *chiles jalapeños en escabeche*

A small bowl
   6 *chiles pasillas,*
     toasted and cleaned
     (see page 30)
Hot water to cover

Cover the chilies with hot water and leave them to soak for about 20 minutes.

A frying pan
   2 *chorizos*
  ½ pound potatoes,
     cooked, skinned,
     and diced

Meanwhile, skin and crumble the *chorizos* and put them to cook over a very low flame. When the fat begins to render out, add the potatoes and stir until they are lightly browned. Remove from the heat and keep warm.

A blender
The soaked chilies
   2 cloves garlic, peeled
1½ cups water
 ¾ teaspoon salt

Drain the chilies, transfer to the blender jar, and blend with the other ingredients until smooth.

A frying pan
Peanut or safflower oil to
    a depth of ¼ inch
The tortillas
The sauce
Paper toweling

Heat the oil. Dip the tortillas, one by one, into the sauce—it should just coat them lightly—and fry briefly on both sides. Drain and keep warm.

The warmed serving
    platter
The grated cheese
The chopped onion

Place the enchiladas, doubled over, on the platter and sprinkle liberally with the cheese and onion, leaving enough space between them for alternating rows of beans, *chorizo* and

The refried beans
The *chorizo* and potato
   mixture
The chili strips
The sardines
The lettuce

potato mixture, chili strips, and sardines. Garnish with the lettuce and serve immediately.

A round platter is ideal for this arrangement.

   Incidentally, sardines have become an accepted part of the Mexican kitchen; they are often used as a stuffing for *chiles poblanos* served cold.

Note

The cooking method for the three recipes that follow is slightly different, and since there is no frying stage for the *enchiladas*, warm, freshly made tortillas are called for.

Green Enchiladas (*from Veracruz*)

4 TO 6 SERVINGS

Have ready:

12 freshly made tortillas
 2 cups Guacamole (see page 42 and note below)
A warmed serving dish (ideally 9 × 13½ × 2)
¼ cup roughly chopped parsley
½ cup crumbled, well-salted farmer cheese (about 3 ounces)

A blender
 1 cup cooked fresh or
    canned Mexican
    green tomatoes (if
    canned, drained
    and blended
    with ⅓ cup water
    and a pinch of
    sugar) (see page 25)
½ cup cooking liquid
    from the tomatoes
    (or water if canned
    tomatoes are used)
 4 *chiles poblanos,*

Blend the green tomatoes with the rest of the ingredients until smooth.

peeled and cleaned
(see page 30) or 5
canned, peeled
green chilies
⅓ medium onion
1 teaspoon salt

A frying pan
  2 tablespoons peanut
     or safflower oil
½ cup sour cream, either
     commercial or
     homemade (see
     page 27)

Heat the oil and cook the sauce over a fairly high flame for about 5 minutes, stirring and scraping the bottom of the pan almost constantly. Remove from the heat and add the sour cream, then set the sauce over a very low flame just to heat it through. Set aside and keep warm.

The tortillas
The sauce
The *guacamole*
The warmed serving dish
A little water or milk
The chopped parsley
The farmer cheese

If the tortillas are not freshly made and still warm, heat them briefly in a steamer (see note page 33). Dip them, one by one, into the sauce, put about 1½ tablespoons of the *guacamole* across the face of each, roll up loosely, and place side by side in the serving dish. Dilute the remaining sauce with a little water or milk and pour over the *enchiladas*. Garnish and serve immediately.

Follow the recipe for *guacamole* on page 42, leaving out the coriander and chilies—the green *enchilada* sauce is sufficiently *picante* for most tastes, and coriander does not go well with the parsley garnish.

Because of the *guacamole*, this is obviously a dish that will not hold, so it must be served as soon as it is assembled. The sauce can be made well ahead, but for best results the *guacamole*, as always, should be made at the last moment.

In Mexico *queso fresco* would be used for the garnish.

Green Enchiladas (*from Central Mexico*)

4 TO 6 SERVINGS

Have ready:

12 freshly made tortillas
1½ to 2 cups cooked, shredded, and well-salted chicken (see page 56)
A warmed serving dish (ideally 9 × 13½ × 2)
⅓ cup crumbled, well-salted farmer cheese (about 2 ounces)
½ medium onion, finely chopped
½ cup Prepared Sour Cream (see page 27)

A blender
  1 cup cooked fresh or canned, drained Mexican green tomatoes (see page 25)
  3 *chiles poblanos*, peeled and cleaned, (see page 30) or 5 canned, peeled green chilies
  2 sprigs coriander, leaves only
  ½ cup shelled, unsalted peanuts
  1 teaspoon salt
  ⅓ cup chicken broth

Blend the green tomatoes with the rest of the ingredients until smooth.

A frying pan
  2 tablespoons peanut or safflower oil

Heat the oil and fry the sauce over a fairly high flame for 5 minutes, stirring and scraping the bottom of the pan almost constantly.

  ½ cup chicken broth

Add the broth and bring to a boil, then remove from the heat and keep warm.

The tortillas
The sauce
The shredded chicken
The warmed serving dish
Broth or water as necessary
The garnish (see above)

If the tortillas are not freshly made and still warm, heat them briefly in a steamer (see note page 33). Dip them, one by one, into the sauce, fill each one with a little of the chicken, roll loosely, and set side by side in the serving dish. Reheat the remaining sauce, diluting it if necessary with a little broth or water. Pour it over the *enchiladas*, garnish with the farmer cheese, onion, and sour cream and serve.

Entomatados

This is a simple dish from Oaxaca that is generally served alone as a "pasta" or "dry soup" course, but it makes an excellent and interesting accompaniment to plainly cooked meats, chicken, or fish.

Have ready:

12 tortillas, warm and freshly made, if possible
A warmed shallow serving dish (about 12 × 7)
  2 tablespoons finely chopped parsley
  ¾ cup crumbled, well-salted farmer cheese
  1 medium onion, thinly sliced

1¼ pounds tomatoes, broiled (see page 29), or 2½ cups canned, drained
3 to 4 *chiles serranos* or any hot, fresh green chilies, lightly broiled with the tomatoes
  1 clove garlic, peeled
  ¾ teaspoon salt, or to taste

Blend the tomatoes with the rest of the ingredients.

A frying pan
  2 tablespoons peanut or safflower oil
  1 clove garlic, peeled and finely chopped
  ⅓ medium onion, finely chopped
The tortillas

Heat the oil and gently fry the onion and garlic, without browning, until soft. Add the tomato puree and cook over a fairly high flame for about 5 minutes, stirring it well from time to time. If the tortillas are not freshly made and still warm, then heat them briefly in a steamer (see note page 33).

The sauce
The warmed serving dish
A little water or broth
The garnish (see above)

Dip them, one by one, into the tomato sauce, fold them over into fours and place, overlapping slightly, in the serving dish. Dilute the remaining sauce if necessary, heat through, and pour over the tortillas. Garnish with the parsley, farmer cheese, and sliced onion and serve immediately.

Indios Vestidos

6 SERVINGS

"Dressed Indians" is the whimsical name of this dish, and sometimes it is known as "little Indians." It's rather like a simple version of *chiles rellenos*, only instead of chilies, tortillas are used. They can be stuffed with either shredded meat or cheese.

Have ready:

12 tortillas, cut into halves
 1 pound pork, cooked, shredded, and well-seasoned (see page 56) or ½ pound farmer cheese (about 1½ cups), crumbled and salted
A large warmed serving platter
 1 large avocado, thinly sliced (see page 16)
 4 tablespoons finely grated Romano or Sardo cheese

A frying pan 2 tablespoons peanut or safflower oil ½ medium onion, finely chopped A blender 1¼ pounds tomatoes, broiled (see page 29) or 2 cups canned, drained 1 canned *chile chipotle* (optional) ½ teaspoon salt, or to taste	Heat the oil and fry the onion gently until soft but not brown. Blend the tomatoes with the chili, then add to the pan, along with the salt. Cook the sauce over a fairly high flame for about 3 minutes, so that it reduces a little. Remove from the heat and keep warm.
The tortilla halves The meat or cheese Toothpicks ½ cup all-purpose flour, approximately	Put a little of the filling onto each piece of tortilla. Fold in half and fasten with a toothpick, then dust lightly with flour.
A frying pan Peanut or safflower oil to a depth of ½ inch A mixing bowl 5 large eggs, separated	Heat the oil. Meanwhile, beat the egg whites and salt until stiff but not dry, then add the yolks, one by one, and continue beating until they are well

½ teaspoon salt
Paper toweling
The warmed serving
   platter
The sauce, heated
The sliced avocado
The grated cheese

incorporated. Dip the tortilla "packages" into the beaten egg—they should be lightly but well coated—and fry until golden brown. Drain well, then put onto the serving platter, pour the heated sauce over, garnish, and serve immediately.

When the *indios* have been fried in the batter, they could be held on a baking sheet, with plenty of paper toweling underneath, in a 350-degree oven for about 20 minutes. The batter will become a little sodden, but then it does under the sauce anyway.

If you are using defrosted tortillas and have trouble with folding them over, steam them first to make them more pliable (see page 33).

Sources for Mexican Ingredients

The list that follows is not meant to be all-inclusive. You will find that many of the ingredients called for in this book can be found on the shelves of many supermarkets and neighborhood stores throughout the country.

Albuquerque

Valley Distributing Co.
2819 2nd Street N.W.
Albuquerque, New Mexico 87107
A wide variety of dried chilies and Mexican ingredients; mail orders.

Atlanta

Rinconcito Latino
Ansley Square Mall
1492B Piedmont Avenue N.E.
Atlanta, Georgia 30309
(Tel: 912 874–3724)
Masa harina, dried chilies (limited variety), canned chilies, etc.

Boston area

Garcia Superette
367 Centre Avenue
Jamaica Plain
Boston, Massachusetts 02130
(Tel: 617 524–1521)
A wide range of Mexican dried chilies, produce, canned goods, and other ingredients; mail orders.

Star Market
625 Mt. Auburn Street
Cambridge, Massachusetts 02238
(Tel: 617 491–3000)

Stop and Shop
390 D Street
East Boston, Massachusetts 02228
(Tel: 617 463–7000)
Both markets carry a limited number of canned Mexican goods and some tropical produce.

Chicago

La Casa del Pueblo
1810 Blue Island
Chicago, Illinois 60608
A large Mexican supermarket that stocks fresh and dried chilies and other ingredients.

Casa Esterio
2719 West Division
Chicago, Illinois 60622
Dried and fresh chilies and many other Mexican ingredients.

Casa Cardenas
324 South Halsted
Chicago, Illinois 60606
(Tel: 312 726–9525 and 312 332–8467)
The largest range of Mexican produce—dried chilies of every type used here, canned and dry ingredients—to be found in the United States.

Claremont (California) area

Many large supermarkets carry a variety of Mexican ingredients, fresh produce, and both corn and wheat-flour tortillas. Seville orange trees line many streets, and banana trees can be found in many back yards for those interested in Yucatecan cooking.

The same probably applies to many cities and small towns in California.

Denver

Safeway Supermarket
2660 Federal Boulevard
Denver, Colorado
A limited range of Mexican ingredients, including fresh green chilies (*serranos*, *jalapeños*, and *poblanos*), Mexican green green tomatoes.

Casa Herrera
2049 Larimer Street
Denver, Colorado 80205

Johnnie's Market
2030 Larimer Street
Denver, Colorado 80205

El Progreso
2282 Broadway (near corner Larimer)
Denver, Colorado 80205
(Tel: 303 623–0576)
All carry a variety of dried chilies, cooking equipment, dry and canned Mexican ingredients, and fresh produce.

Fresno

Chihuahua Tortilleria
718 F Street
Fresno, California 93706

Houston

Rice Food Market
3700 Navigation (at Everton)
Houston, Texas 77003
Fresh chilies and Mexican produce of all types, some dried chilies (*ancho*, *guajillo*, more rarely *mulato*), Mexican dry and canned goods.

Most of the larger Rice and Weingarten markets carry fresh produce and a more limited range of Mexican ingredients. There are many small Mexican groceries in the Navigation Boulevard area that carry a small selection of ingredients.

Antone's Import Co.
807 Taft, 8111 South Main, 1639 South Voss Road
Houston, Texas
All three branches carry some dried chilies, canned goods, corn husks, whole spices, etc.

Los Angeles

El Mercado
First Avenue and Lorena
East Los Angeles, California 90063
Like a Mexican open market, with many stands selling fresh and dried chilies, cooking utensils, canned goods.

Modesto (California)

Don Juan Foods
1715 Crows Landing Road
Modesto, California 95351

New York City

DOWNTOWN

Casa Moneo
210 West 14th Street
New York, New York 10014
(Tel: 212 929–1644)
Large variety of Mexican ingredients, including canned goods, dried chilies, *chorizos*, spices, and cooking equipment; mail orders.

MIDTOWN

Trinacria Importing Co.
415 Third Avenue
New York, New York 10016
(Tel: 212 LE2–5567)
Mexican canned goods, occasionally fresh green chilies, fresh coriander, spices.

H. Roth and Son
968 Second Avenue,
New York, New York 10022
(Tel: 212 RE4–1110)

Mexican canned chilies and green tomatoes, spices, etc. For mail orders write H. Roth and Sons, 1577 First Avenue, New York, New York 10028

UPTOWN (West)

Perello, Inc.
2585 Broadway
New York, New York 10025
(Tel: 212 MO6–0901)
Masa harina, canned chilies, fresh coriander

The Magic Carpet West
201 West 98th Street
New York, New York 10025
(Tel: 212 222–2189)
Open for retail trade Friday, Saturday, 10 to 6 P.M.
Mexican canned chilies, dried chilies, plus a large range of spices, sesame seeds, Mexican green tomatoes.

UPTOWN (East)

La Marqueta
Park Avenue between 112th and 116th
　　Stand 499, at 114th Street

Almost always fresh green chilies from Mexico (*serranos* or *jalapeños*) and sometimes *poblanos*.

Stands 461 and 462 (between 114th and 115th Streets) Coriander and *chiles habañeros* all year round.

Oakland (California)

Mi Rancho
464 Seventh Street
Oakland, California 94607

Salinas (California)

Sal-Rex Foods
258 Griffin Street
Salinas, California 93901

Saint Louis

Soulard Market
Some fresh chilies and coriander, whole spices.

900 Geyer Street
(Sr. Jesus Lagunas)
(Tel: 314 231–3036)
Masa harina, chiles anchos, tortilla presses, canned Mexican goods, etc.

San Antonio

Frank Pizzini
202 Produce Row
San Antonio, Texas 78207
(Tel: 512 CA7–2082)
Dried chilies, spices, dried herbs; mail orders
　　Both the open market and small produce stands on Produce Row have a year-round supply of fresh Mexican produce. The larger supermarkets in the area carry some produce and other Mexican ingredients, tortillas, etc.

San Diego

Some of the larger supermarkets and small markets, especially in the National Avenue area, carry a great variety of Mexican produce, canned goods, tortillas, etc., but the real *aficionados* will take the trouble to go across the border to the market area in Tijuana, where everything is available—especially good tortillas and *queso fresco* from the *tortilleria* near the market.

San Francisco

La Palma
2884 24th Street
San Francisco, California 94110
(Tel: 415 MI8-5500)
Fresh and dried chilies, fresh Mexican green tomatoes, canned goods, spices.

Mi Rancho Market
3365 20th Street
San Francisco, California 94110

Santa Barbara

Villareal Market
728 East Haley Street
Santa Barbara, California 93101
(Tel: 904 963–2613)
A wide variety of fresh and dried chilies, cooking utensils, canned goods, *chorizos*, fresh tortillas.

Santa Cruz Market
605 North Milpas Street
Santa Barbara, California 93101
A very wide variety of dried chilies and Mexican cheeses, among many other ingredients.

La Tolteca
614 East Haley Street
Santa Barbara, California 93101
Fresh *masa* and tortillas.

Santa Fe

Theo. Roybal Store
Rear 212, 214, 216 Galisteo Street
Santa Fe, New Mexico 87501
Herbs, cooking utensils, spices, many Mexican ingredients; mail orders.

Washington, D.C.

La Sevillana
2469 18th Street N.W.
Washington, D.C. 20009
A limited range of dried chilies, canned goods, and other Mexican ingredients.

Safeway International
1110 F. Street N.W.
Washington, D.C. 20004
(Tel: 202 628–1880)
A large variety of basic ingredients for Mexican cooking, canned and dry goods, fresh chilies, etc.

Casa Peña
1636 17th Street N.W.
Washington, D.C. 20009
(Tel: 202 462–2222)

What in the World (a branch of Casa Peña)
5441 MacArthur Blvd. N.W.
Washington, D.C. 20016
(Tel: 202 632–6500)
A large variety of dried and fresh chilies, Mexican green tomatoes, and Mexican canned and dry ingredients.

Bibliography

BELTRAN, LOURDES A. *La Cocina Jarocha*. Mexico City: Editorial Pax-Mexico, 1960.

CALLEJA, TERESA, and SESTO, GLORIA. *La Cocinera Poblana*. Mexico City: El Libro Español, 1950.

————. *La Cocina Poblana*. Mexico City: Ediciones Cicerón, S.A., 1954.

ESCAMILLA, ADELA ROMO. *La Cocina de Doña Adela*. Mexico City: Compañía Editorial Continental, S.A., 1944.

LEÓN, JOSEFINA VELÁZQUEZ DE. *Cocina de Aguascalientes*. Mexico City: Editorial Velázquez de León, 1957.

————. *Cocina de la Comarca Lagunera*. Mexico City: Editorial Velázquez de León, 1957.

————. *Cocina de Guanajuato*. Mexico City: Editorial Velázquez de León, n.d.

————. *Cocina de Nuevo León*. Mexico City: Editorial Velázquez de León, n.d.

————. *Cocina Oaxaqueña*. Mexico City: Editorial Velázquez de León, n.d.

————. *Cocina de San Luís*. Mexico City: Editorial Velázquez de León, 1957.

————. *Cocina de Sonora*. Mexico City: Editorial Velázquez de León, 1958.

————. *Cocina Tamaulipeca*. Mexico City: Editorial Velázquez de León, 1957.

————. *Cocina Veracruzana*. Mexico City: Editorial Velázquez de León, 1966.

————. *Cocina de Zacatecas*. Mexico City: Editorial Velázquez de León, n.d.

MADRIGAL, LOLITA. *Libro de Cocina de Doña Lolita*. Mexico City: Editorial Diana, S.A., 1964.

Nuestra Cocina. Comité de Damas Pro Beneficencia Española. Mexico City: Impresiones Modernas, 1962.

RAMOS ESPINOSA, VIRGINIA. *Recetas para la Buena Mesa*. Mexico City: Editorial Jus, S.A., 1953.

Ricas Meriendas y Buffets. Tampico: Antiguos Talleres de Al Libro Mayor, S.A., 1966.

SANCHEZ, MAYO ANTONIO. *Cocina Mexicana*. Mexico City: Editorial Diana, S.A., 1964.

Index

155